Last Words

LAST WORDS:
FREDERICK'S BIONARY

Frederick Blanch

NORTH STAR PRESS OF ST. CLOUD, INC.
St. Cloud, Minnesota

ISBN: 978-0-87839-561-3

First Edition: September 2011

Printed in the United States of America

Published by
North Star Press of St. Cloud, Inc.
P.O. Box 451
St. Cloud, Minnesota 56302
northstarpress.com

DEDICATED

As always, to my two guardian angels
and to
Motoko

First Word

This little opus covers lots of years, spanning bewildering, almost fictional change. Nevertheless, I have aimed for at least a moderate degree of historical accuracy (but do not guarantee bull's-eyes), offering the caveat that advancing age has not improved a steady aiming eye, and that I share the writers' urge for creative amplification—and opinion.

The dictionary-like format evolved because I presume to think of myself as a man of words, which accounts for the enclosed material arranged as a biographical dictionary, a bionary (technically, an onomasticon). I semi-apologize for the gaggle of incomplete sentences, tense violations, excessive passive voice, overwrought alliteration, infinitives split to smithereens, etc. And, writer or not, if a cliché best describes something, I use it, no apologies. Nonetheless, as this literary intransigence stumbles across the pages, it is my sincere wish that it brings enjoyment to the reader.

The author, pre-curmudgeon

A

abdomen — A secret I try to keep hidden beneath my belt. As I mature, I fear my secret has been somewhat compromised by malfunctioning belts.

ability — Like a satchel of money, I never would have objected to having more.

abnormal — I always had plenty of that.

abroad — I have been there . . . and known a few.

absurd — An editorial term. I have a morbid fear that it will be applied to my literary products.

abut — Dad regularly urged me to get off of mine and "do something useful!"

accident — Mother informed me at an early age that I was one of these. My parents were married but times were hard and extra mouths swallowed precious resources. Her revelation was an adroit Introduction to Protestant Guilt. All good children of the Depression Era were required to learn it and I have been "Protestant-ing" ever since.

accomplice — Those who have helped me edit a script.

across — What I have had to bear for expressing the truth . . . as I see it.

adrift — Big white messes having no purpose or direction. Common to Minnesota winters, they make me yearn for Costa Rican Rain Forests where I can photograph beautiful flowers and birds without getting rigged up like an Eskimo.

adultery — Though I suffer from arthritis and other plagues of aging, I still think adultery is more fun than infancy. But maybe that's just because I'm an old guy and can't remember much further back than yesterday.

advertising — A business I was in for a few years. It came as the result of my silkscreen printing business: Screencraft. As a sign peddler, I completely lost patience watching customers write their advertising copy "peas & carrots." They couldn't all be selling ampersands, could they? So, when I suggested they try "PEAS & CARROTS," I hit the minor big-time in the ad biz—that means I made a little money.

advice — No matter how much I have given . . . and, in this area, my generosity is notorious, the ungrateful world is still not a better place. I'm beginning to believe that instead of just squandering it, I should have saved some for myself.

affair — A couple.

affluence — Not much of this . . . but plenty of effluence.

afoul — My ear tells me afoul could be a squat bird noted for its tasty qualities when Southern fried. Yet, memory defines it for me as a specific incident of running afoul of the law, in the early winter of 1960. At the time, like Mr. Bumble in Oliver Twist, I thought the law was "an ass."

Though the situation had its origins some months prior, it began for me around supper time on a cold day in January or February — I don't remember which. Two large Minneapolis policemen knocked on the apartment door and informed me that I was under arrest. Flabbergasted, I had not the slightest notion of what I had done–no recent crimes sprang to mind: no robberies, no burglaries, murders, or assaults. I could not even recall the last time I'd spit on the sidewalk.

The arresting officers were pleasant fellows. Without seeming too judgmental, they explained that the warrant outlined the heinous offense of an overdue parking ticket. Nowadays, I read and hear about folks with long strings of traffic violations, multiple drunk driving convictions, and the like, that seem to go unpunished — but back then, gulags flourished and crimes against humanity were called to reckoning. The smaller of the enforcers (only a behemoth) hauled out glinting handcuffs but was stayed by his larger sidekick.

"If you ain't got twenty-five bucks for bail on ya, scrape it up now . . . otherwise it's a night in the can."

I was dumbfounded. I was headed to jail for a ticket I couldn't have gotten. "But that's impossible officer . . . and I don't have twenty-five dollars." I carried no folding money . . . every dime, literally, went back into my silk screen printing business.

"Let's cuff 'im and get going," the officer in charge of metal restraints urged.

"Let's give 'im uh chance t'come up with it." He then asked me, "An' why ain't it possible ya got a ticket? Yer wagon, same license number's sittin' right outside."

"Because I keep a special account, I . . ." There was no use explaining it to the cop, I switched to the bail money. "Can I ask around . . . for the cash?" I lived in a four-plex and hoped that the landlady, who lived downstairs, would help.

"Yeah, make it snappy though." The big cop could tell his partner was getting anxious to get Minneapolis's newest Public Enemy Number One into irons.

I ran downstairs, borrowed the cash, was cuffed, and inserted into the back seat of a squad car, which, thankfully, had been left running and was warm. My memory is a fickle thing; I remember every detail of my apprehension and the fingerprinting procedure, but have absolutely no recollection of how I got back home from the courthouse. I do remember that I went downstairs and properly thanked my landlady for the loan and then went back to work until about three in the morning. But the story doesn't end there.

Attorney Smith, a sort of friend, shook his head as I explained that I could have paid the ticket and a late fee, but that I had never received the ticket and I didn't want a record of ignoring one. And, anyway, the date for my court appearance was already set.

"I've got this account and . . ."

Lawyer Smith interrupted, "You sure you really didn't get the ticket? You're being truthful with me?"

"I'm very sure and I sure as hell wouldn't lie to my lawyer!"

"That isn't much of a defense." He leaned back and rubbed his chin. "I've got a guy I've worked with before, Boots Ottenfield . . . a detective . . . he's good with a lie detector."

"Thought they didn't count in court."

"There's nothing preventing us from bringing it up . . . if it turns out you're truthful," his voice betrayed skepticism, "he could even testify."

I remember sitting in a dark little room hooked to a machine with a roll of paper on it. Attorney Smith's friend spent less than five minutes asking me questions—one was: "Have you ever cheated on your wife?" Due to fortunate life-experience timing, my answer was a truthful "No." I vividly recall that he never asked me a question that made me lie.

Back in the lawyer's office, Smith informed me that the best the detective could say about the test was that it was "inconclusive." He confided that Detective Ottenfield was pretty sure I'd lied about everything. I concluded that Ottenfield figured everyone cheated on his wife and a guy that couldn't own up to it was a died-in-the-wool liar. Though my attorney didn't say so, I got the impression that he, as well as my test examiner, thought I was the most untruthful thing since Pinocchio. I half expected him to inquire if my nose had lengthened lately.

" . . . So we better not refer to the lie test in court," he said.

"Well, I still got this checking . . ."

A hand wave silenced me. "We don't have diddle, but maybe we'll draw a good judge," said Smith.

Lady Luck seemed determined to ignore me—guess I wasn't going to cheat on my wife with her—I drew Minneapolis Traffic Court's infamous "hanging judge," Tom Bergin. Rumors of his savagery were legend: a man charged for disturbing the peace—slammed his car door in front of a mortuary—was hanged and his remains sent to a leper colony as mulch for their broccoli bed. Of course I really didn't believe that he had sentenced his own mother to twenty years hard labor . . . for j-walking . . . in the ally behind her house. A shaken lawyer Smith advised me to just plead guilty and pray; I think he was terrified of the judge.

The court experience was not without its moments of levity. The case immediately before mine involved about a dozen young men, in their late teens or early twenties. It seems they were riding in two cars that drove alongside each other while the occupants exchanged insults. They not only blocked traffic on a busy street, but impeded a police car, which led to a drive down to traffic court. They and their attorneys made quite a crowd as all gathered in a knot before the lofty judicial bench. It was a silent group except for one young man who, loudly and persistently, interrupted Judge Bergin's stern lecture by proclaiming, "I object!" Each outburst elicited a wave of snickers from the spectators. The judge rapped his gavel, louder and louder, as the "I object" interruptions kept coming.

Finally, belying his fearsome reputation, Judge Bergin sighed and addressed the fellow. "Well," he snapped, "what is it? What's your objection?"

"I object to being here!"

The gavel smashed down again and again, but was no deterrent to the laughter and general uproar in the courtroom. The judge allowed himself a fleeting smile and waited out the merriment. An explanation followed, officialdom had collared a boy with no connection to the case.

Then my turn came, People of Minneapolis vs. Frederick Blanch. That seemed like an awfully lopsided contest. Smith launched into unintelligible gibberish. Judge Bergin's gaze drifted down to somewhere in the vicinity of his feet. I supposed he was looking for the book he intended to throw at me. I tugged at Smith's suit coattail.

"Please. Sit down," I whispered. Then I stood and said, "Your honor, may I speak?"

"Your attorney lost his voice?"

"I fired him." There was restless stirring by my side — dismissed attorneys do that — and the judge glared down like I'd be lucky if that book he was about to throw at me wasn't wrapped in cobras.

"You're asking this court to represent yourself?"

I think the translation of his question ran something like, "You want to put your head in the noose with no one to help cut the rope?"

"Yes, sir."

"Go ahead, then . . ." he allowed, but under his breath, still plenty loud enough for me to hear, he added, " . . . morning's been a goddamn circus anyway."

"I keep this special checking account," I said, waving a little green covered check register. "It's for nothing but parking tickets."

"Gimme." The judge crooked his finger and the clerk arose, took the record from me, and handed it up to His Honor.

It covered a period of six or eight months and contained a listing of twenty or so checks. The single payee was the City of Minneapolis.

Judge Bergin glanced at it and said, "Explain."

"I call on a lot of advertising agencies . . . sometimes they keep me waiting for a couple of hours, other customers do too. I know it's not a deductible business expense . . . for taxes, but I keep track anyway. Far as I'm concerned, it's a business expense like any other."

Judge Bergin shook his head. "Never heard of such a goofy thing." He picked up a file folder and, wetting a finger on his tongue, picked through the papers. "You claiming you never got the ticket, uh . . . dated October fourteenth?"

"That's right."

"We send out a reminder, you know." He studied the file intently. "Warning went out on . . . Thursday, December fourteenth. Maybe that explains it," he said absently; his voice dropped. "Post office . . . holidays . . . you never been at . . ." He read an address.

I recognized the downtown area. "I think that's by Peavey Milling's office."

"Anybody besides you drive your vehicle?"

The light bulb in my head blinked on. Why hadn't I thought of that before? "Yes, sir, my employees use it occasionally . . . for deliveries. I hadn't thought of it before but we delivered an order of custom Christmas cards to Peavey in mid October."

"That's good enough for me . . . you still owe on the ticket, but the penalty fine is waved." The gavel banged, "Case dismissed."

Ah, vindication! Was it sweet? Almost.

Though I'd dodged the gallows, Attorney Smith was no longer even "sort of" a friend and I'd spent time and money I could ill afford. However, at that point in my life I felt it was important that my reputation as a law-abider flourish. From this side of my life, I realize that I should have just paid the fine and forgotten about it — but then, I wouldn't have this treasured memory. However, contemplating the memory of this little drama suggests to me that perhaps the law wasn't the only ass involved.

after glow — The brilliant light one experiences after reading one of my manuscripts . . . if promptly thrown in the fireplace.

agent — I've occasionally given this a try, but there's not much call for Gentlemen anymore. I have no knowledge of the other kind, writers' representatives, who have generally avoided me.

agitator — Many writers lay claim to stirring up emotions in others. Like Thomas Paine's, Common Sense. If I had any common sense, I'd quit inflicting pain with my writing and get a job in an Insomnia Clinic where they give pats on the back for writing that stirs up yawns.

agreement — This is my long suit (as we card players like to say) . . . especially when the other guy does the agreeing.

aggressive — This little anecdote about the word aggressive needs sound to effectively convey its point, but I'll try and work without it. It has provided me with many smiles over the past fifty plus years and served as a primer on how people see themselves verses how they really behave.

About a year after starting Screencraft, I hired a fellow to build an office in the building I had taken over. Sometime during that first year, I'd visited a large office supply company that assigned one of their salesmen to me, Jim Cole. When he discovered that I would eventually have a need for office furniture, he made sporadic "sales" calls. His invariable opening line ran something like, "I suppose you'll be wanting office furniture one of these days." I just as invariably responded, "Yes, I will." I still remember the man but for all the wrong business reasons. I remember him because he never could drum up the courage to simply ask me to buy anything.

It took six or eight months to construct my office because I'd hired a fellow (a paint-mixer in a competitor's shop) who came in two nights a week to work on it. During that time, Jim probably made at least a dozen stops, hinting that he was in the office products business. He was a time-waster for me, but, as I made my living selling, I made a practice to always see salespeople who took the trouble to make in-person calls.

As my office was taking final shape, a very young fellow (I was an elder statesman of twenty-nine years) from another office furniture company stopped by and made a very convincing pitch for his brand of desks, and other furniture. When he asked for the order, I said, "Sure."

(In fact as I write this story, I am sitting in the very chair, at the very desk that nice young man sold me in 1959.)

I guess my seeming lack of interest in purchasing an office suite discouraged Mr. Cole; whatever the reason, his calls had stopped before I finally bought my office furnishings. It was at least a couple of years before I met Jim on the street in downtown Minneapolis. After exchanging banalities, he made the toughest sales pitch I'd ever heard from him: "You ever buy any office furniture?"

"Yeah, Jim, I did," then I added, "from a real nice . . . aggressive kid."

Jim swallowed. He obviously wanted to respond. I could almost see the wheels turning in his head. In a drawn-out, drawling whine he said, "Geeeee, Fer . . . red . . . we're uh-gress-ive tooooo."

agriculture — The agrarian culture of my early days. Though spending but a few (albeit formative) years in the little farm town of Claremont, Minnesota, it remains my spiritual home. However, you couldn't bribe or beat me into living there now — or ever again. The "agri" excepted, there is more "culture" in a dirty petri dish than in all of Claremont.

airlift — The boost my money will give to beneficiaries when I croak.

alimony — The money I've had the misfortune to know . . . but briefly.

almost — An adverb that, uncomfortably, applies to the success of my musical and literary efforts. For me, its synonym is "close but not quite." I never wanted to settle for close, which accounts for my lack of interest in the sport of horseshoes.

allergy — I'm allergic to grass pollen and dust to a small degree and, to a large degree, myself.

alliteration — Patently possessing a paucity of perspicacity, I'm a pathetically paltry practitioner, principally provoking pitiless pooh-poohs and put-downs. A versified exemplar, of my perpetration, follows:

Falconry

If words could perch upon the arm
Before release in deadly stoop,
Or simply hooded, ere they harm,
What fortunes might we then recoup?

And were discoursive beaks restrained
Or raptored words were thonged from slight,
If taloned, tiercel tongues were tamed,
What doves might soar in peaceful flight?

allowance — Until I began to earn my own spending money, Dad came through with ten cents a week; usually two nickels. If I listened to them closely, I could still hear the buffalos bellowing — probably from being pinched so hard.

alphabetical — I have selected wives in alphabetical order: Beverly, JoAnn, & Motoko. Thank God, I've gotten through the M's! That means it's all downhill from here, I'm halfway finished — unless I start again with Alice.

alphorn — An alphornist commissioned me to write a piece for alphorn and three (French) horns. It was premiered at the 1993 Zummerfest, outdoors, next to Symphony Hall in Minneapolis. By a stroke of fortune (to what extent is controlled by point-of-view), an ambulance service chose that precise time to test their sirens. For three out of the five minutes required for *Alptitudinous*, an unbidden chorus of mechanical wailing joined my opus. The sirens, combined with the tumultuous churning of adjacent fountains prevented the musicians from hearing each other and the audience from hearing my piece. Thus was my musical reputation preserved for another day.

anniversary — For its One-hundredth Anniversary Season, Thursday Musical, a Minnesota classical music organization, chose six or seven Minnesota composers to feature during their year-long presenting cycle. As my contribution, they selected the third and fourth movements from my cello quartet, Quattro Voce for Cello — it was the only piece from the featured composers selected for further broadcast by the venerable arts radio station, WCAL, since slain by its unscrupulous rival, KSJN.

anus — A term of endearment, generally used in its colloquial form, that has been directed to me by friends, acquaintances, and more than a few strangers.

appearances — My office walls are a photographic jungle of exotically colored birds and flowers from faraway beaches, rainforests, and mountains. One of two home-grown exceptions is the large, single frame of three eight-by-ten photographs of my (then) eleven year old daughter, Susan, hosting an alfresco tea party with her friends, Gretel and Winkie. It must have been a formal affair because both dogs are dressed for the occasion. Her guests are "mostlys" — mostly shepherd with a solid mix of unknown antecedents. Susan frequently dressed

Susan, Gretel, and Winkie

her living dolls in scarves, aprons, and sometimes pants and shirts; therein, lies this story about appearances.

It took a couple of years, working many Saturdays and some afternoons, to complete the quarter-mile fence fronting the township road, which, when finished, would encircle our Wright County property. I dug the postholes with a hand digger and spent lots more time (and sweat) on the project than I would have preferred. However, the onerous task was not without a memorable moment of comedy. On a very hot spring day, I heard the gravelly crunch of tires moving slowly along our township road. Simultaneously, I noticed Winkie, in full regalia of shirt and shorts, one of my red and silver regimental striped ties trailing over her back, racing down the hill toward the oncoming vehicle. She was an incurable chaser, the primary reason for the fence, and she was determined that no wheeled machine would pass her territory unchallenged.

I stood on a low hill, affording a clear view of an elderly couple in the approaching car. The passenger, a gray-haired woman, pointed at the apparition gliding low across the ground at an incredible speed, the look on her face quickly changed from wonder to terror. The driver, a septuagenarian at least, must have shared her reaction as, suddenly, the Buick spewed a volley of gravel from its rear tires, and fishtailing violently, sped toward the county highway. Swerving onto the macadam, engine roaring, screeching tires smoking, the automobile disappeared in a cloud of blue-white exhaust. I nearly choked with laughter and immediately ran up to the house to tell Susan and JoAnn about our frightful "monster."

The following Monday, when JoAnn returned from her duties in the County Attorney's office, she reported that one of the Sheriff's deputies, acting on a concerned citizen's report, stopped by and inquired if we were keeping any "peculiar children."

"I explained what happened," she said, "and about Sue and her dress-ups on the dogs."

"What'd he say?"

"Not much, just that 'Appearances can be deceiving.'"

Amen.

art—I admit to being a beholder of beauty and art with less than 20-20 vision. However, I'm sure some of my "beholdings" have contributed to my cataracts.

arthritis—see beekeeping

ascent—Starting out, I obeyed the adage: a penny saved is a penny earned and saved my pennies. A cent here and a cent there and before I knew it, I had a bag of one cent pieces which the mere thought of lifting, threatened a double hernia—and wouldn't have bought more than a decent meal. Then I decided to give myself a raise—by saving dollars.

author—What I see when I look in the mirror. Must remember to donate that thing to a fun-house.

authoritarian—Dear old Dad's middle name. And, if he'd had any sense of consistency, he'd have gone to court and made it his surname too.

B

backfire — An interesting word. At about age fifteen, I spent a summer fighting forest fires in the Klamath National Forest (Northern California & Southern Oregon) and learned a little about the efficacy of setting backfires. Not one to ignore such instructive life-lessons, I've set quite a few of them myself — that have usually backfired!

bachelor's degree — A temperature I never reached because of my constant marital status.

bacilli — Rod-like organisms affecting the brains of those deeming my witty comebacks silly.

backhand — One of the very few things generously bestowed upon me by my father . . . though he never did come up with a racquet. He knew that after a good backhand, he could count on me to supply the racket.

badinage — Webster's II defines as light, playful banter. I've often wondered, if I tried bantering lighter and more playfully, could it be classified as goodinage, or at least, betterinage. You don't need to dwell on it, I know both those "inages" are bad.

beekeeper — During the second winter of my fifteen year sojourn in the country (in Wright County, south of Annandale), I made the mistake of reading a book on beekeeping. The dry tinder of my mind kindles too readily and, therefore, by spring, I had already built three hive sets and ordered three packages of bees, complete with queens in their own little cages. In no time, I was in free fall over the precipice of my latest pursuit and running several hundred colonies of bees, many of which were stationed several miles distant, the furthest in a clover field in the shadow of the cooling towers of the Becker power plant in Sherburne County. Of course, I had to build a sanitary honey house (which I constructed inside my pole-barn) complete with stainless steel dewaxing, extracting, clarifying, and bottling equipment. I had watched over enough shoulders during my home construction to muddle through the necessary plumbing, electric, and carpentry work. The single project glitch was the sawing off a scarcely noticeable tip of a finger.

Dear German-shepherd-friend, Rocky, was a constant by-my-side companion throughout every step of the beekeeping venture. The only exceptions came when hauling equipment to and from off-premise locations and on sales calls (when he preferred to ride in the back of the pickup truck). He maintained a reasonable, but nonetheless proximate distance when I removed honey supers, seeming to realize that I, as honey plunderer-in-chief, would be the primary target of *Apis melliferan* reprisal. Independent of me, he maintained a far greater distance to the beeyard, especially on mornings following a nighttime sally against the bees by skunks; outraged nectar gatherers savaged anything in fur closer than a hundred yards for a couple of days or more after each raid.

The beeyard was a level field of about an acre separated from the house by a windbreak of several rows of trees. Nonetheless, skunks left their unmistakable calling card that filled the air for a half-mile in all directions, effortlessly proclaiming their predations through closed windows and doors. On those occasions, Rocky would settle down by the back door while I checked the damage. Skunks might eat honey, but their foremost interest was bees. I spent a few nights watching the hives, and as far as I could discern, the smelly little fellows would scratch at the entrance and eat the guards as they emerged. Unchecked, this could markedly reduce hive populations, hence, honey production.

Trapping might have reduced the numbers of aromatic pillagers, but whether because of unwillingness to use traps or plain old indolence, I let nature handle the problem. We had nesting pairs of horned owls on the property and skunk was high on their menu. My attitude? Bon appetite.

Though not originally intending to commercialize my hobby, I had to do something with all that delicious product. That led to Merry Meadow Farms, which was our honey brand. Years in the corrugated board business by proxy (Screencraft printed and die-cut tons of the stuff for retail in-store displays) provided the experience to design a container that was mailable, made a nice gift-box because of its simulated walnut covering, and served as a stand-alone retail display. These boxes, accommodating a one-pound jar, were packed, a dozen to a carton. They sold as premiums, Christmas gifts and the like, mostly to businesses. As a rule, honey supports neither pathogenic microorganisms nor, as a consequence, lawyers; this added to its salability. A small, but fancy chain of Twin Cities' grocery stores, Byerly's, maintained a large bakery facility in Rockford and bought basswood honey in bulk.

Basswood trees do not produce large nectar crops every year. Mystifyingly, most of them cooperate in a sort of nectar-festival and manage a major joint bloom every few years. Basswood nectar is the basis for a light "water-white" honey, much prized for its light taste and excellent flavor in pastry products. As bees are quite "source specific" (all hive-mates gathering nectar from a single blooming plant type), beekeepers may assume their honey is a "kind" like clover, wildflower, or basswood, etc.

A special beekeeping bonus for me was the permanent (to date) elimination of arthritis in my fingers. By age forty, my morning ablutions began with running hot water over my nearly inflexible hands. However, a couple of years of beekeeping produced a dramatic, remedial effect, moving my flexible-finger-clock back about twenty years. I wasn't sure if the effect was real, from the fifty or more finger-stings a day when removing honey or the placebo effect from exposure to extreme beekeeper lore—honey cures everything from bedsores to broken hearts. At a rare visit to a doctor, I cannot remember the reason, I mentioned the miraculous renaissance and was promptly informed, "It's all in your head." I felt like I stood before my father, berating me as the "stupidest kid" he'd "ever seen." Never saw that doctor again.

Since then, I have seen pictures of stone carvings originating in Golden Age Greece depicting physicians applying bees to patient's fingers. I suppose that was all in the stone sculptor's head.

All in all, beekeeping was a sweet experience.

bliss—But for a single subject, I have never turned my back on learning. Oddly enough, that single subject abides in the category of those-things-that-are-near-and-dear. For my entire remembered life, I have been fascinated by the beauty of colorful birds—only past middle-age did I add flowers to my repertoire of interests.

During my freshman year at the University of Minnesota (1947-48), the farm campus possessed large tracts of brushy, rolling hills

Blissful Beauty - Red-Headed Trogon

and swampy areas (that would soon be scraped flat to accommodate housing for returning war veterans and their families). However, as that travesty had not yet occurred, the U offered a course in ornithology that utilized their wonderful wildlife area. Given only in the spring quarter, I spent two thirds of the academic year looking forward to alfresco instruction. Soon into the course, I was rudely disabused of its anticipated pleasures. Instead of observing birds and other wildlife in the au naturel area, most course-time sequestered us in a basement classroom. Beautiful feathers and glorious song reduced to dry bones and dryer descriptions threatened to destroy my childish notions of avian beauty; I quit the course cold, while I still could appreciate an idealized vision of ornithological wonders. It was a decision I have never regretted. I wished not the fetters of technical restraint; instead, as a bird on the wing, I have let soar the simple romantic pleasures of absorbing the poetry of feathered color, perhaps demonstrating the adage that ignorance is bliss.

bottom line –In the late 1970s, I became involved in the solar heating business. Our product, Solarmat, composed of parallel glass fibers in mats of varying thickness, could be stuffed into the cavities between construction studs, covered with clear glass sheeting, and, with a plenum at top and bottom, the entire wall of a structure became a solar heat collector. It was a simple concept. It was a promising business.

The 1973 Arab Oil Embargo, fresh in American minds, and escalating energy prices combined to create a receptive climate for the reemergence of the solar heating industry (which had seen extensive use in the 1920s). Our product required no energy eating pumps (which often resulted in net energy loss), no fluids (which had leakage potential), and installed easily, by almost anyone with a minimal mechanical bent. Maintenance crowded nil. And, as an ex silk screen printer, I realized that its surface could carry colorful designs and/or graphics.

Of course, we tried for one of the numerous government grants available to develop solar. However, Solarmat just didn't have enough complicated bells and whistles to interest the grant givers; it simply worked. I thought it quite ironic that the solar collector array on the roof of Honeywell Corporation looked like giant, wilted daisies, their heads hanging down to avoid the very sun's rays they were built to collect. Scuttlebutt amongst small solar providers was that the corporate giant had received a ton of government money to develop solar collectors, most of it spent (squandered?) by traveling to and from a Puerto Rico solar experimental station (mostly in the winter). If that is untrue, I apologize to Honeywell, but only to the extent of any inaccuracy.

I made a sales call on Marlin Grant, president of Marvin H. Anderson Construction Company (then, the largest builder of mass homes in the Twin Cities) who immediately saw Solarmat's potential in new home construction. They built a sample home utilizing the entire sidewall as a solar collector, colored brown to match the house. After a winter's use, Anderson Construction reported that the solar heat collection measured up to our projected calculations.

Handyman magazine (perhaps a couple million circulation at that time) used a picture of the Anderson home for a front cover, plus a nice article, giving our miniscule operation national press. At that very time, major companies tried numerous ploys to convince the public of their concern and efforts to accommodate environmental issues.

I hoped that the Pillsbury Company (which I perceived as a responsible corporate citizen) might be persuaded to let us print some outstanding graphics on Solarmat, and use it in the walls of a Burger King (then a Pillsbury subsidiary). What more startling and practical way to proclaim their efforts to conserve energy? Save money on energy and create an advertising bonanza in one stroke, who could resist that?

A top Pillsbury executive spent an hour or so listening to my presentation. He impressed me with his cordiality and sincerity and his enthusiasm for the project.

So, it's a done deal. Right?

No.

There's just one more little step. "You have to get clearance on it from Mr. . . . He's head of the Division."

I contacted the Division head who agreed that our proposal could potentially save on energy costs, and might be a public relations gold mine. Nonetheless, he declined to pursue the idea, explaining that, as manager of the Division for but a two-year stint, he was responsible for showing a maximum profit. "I can't possibly do that," he said, "it'd ruin my bottom line."

brief—Length of time my humor column, From the Lowlands, appeared in a local newspaper.

business — About twenty years and forty tank-cars of sweat went into my silkscreen printing business, Screencraft. Starting in a broom closet had its advantages: I could reach anything without moving, which resulted in competitive efficiencies. The first couple of years I averaged two or three hours of sleep per night — another advantage of small room size, I couldn't fall over as I slept on the job. However, in spite of space restrictions, the business prospered. Note that the business prospered, not I. As I walked into the shop one afternoon, I couldn't figure out why my shop guys were snickering, until I was told that the seat of my pants was missing. It was my only suit, worn right through the bottom — you wouldn't think a fellow who did that much sitting could be successful. Well, better lucky than smart. Things worked out and I managed to buy a new suit. Dad used to say, "The coat and pants do all the work, but the vest gets all the gravy." Life isn't fair, is it? Good old Screencraft blossomed into several other businesses and before I knew it, I was in gravy up to my knees. However, I was saved from gravy-on-the-knee, as wife number two cleaned me up and out quite nicely.

cancer — In 2004 I was diagnosed with stage-two prostate cancer. My urologist, a surgeon by training, wanted to chop out the offending organ, rendering me free of the lethal growth and definitive gender. He was a little "put-out" that I opted for a different treatment regimen, but what could I do? My clothes-closet bulged with trousers and I really had no room to add skirts. Forty-two radiation treatments (and a couple of inconvenient side-effects) later, have, to date held my unwelcome visitor in check.

chamber music — I scribbled away, producing about one hundred pieces of this stuff. A critic writing for the Westport News (Connecticut) referred to me as "a gifted composer . . . Mr. Blanch has indeed given us a welcome addition to the literature." — I don't know if he is still employed.

Champions — The title of one of my novels.

cliché — Outside of the Gettysburg Address (which is sacrosanct and I dare not point out that "all men are created equal" and "died in vain" might get a red pencil nowadays), I suppose most literary efforts benefit from editorial oversight. This is not a brief for sloppy writing, just letting off a little steam (see how nicely that cliché fits) about the occasional pedantic editor (and some fellow writers) who, with the glee of a hobo finding a ten-dollar bill beneath a park bench, enthusiastically point out that I've used a cliché. Oh, heaven forefend — bad writing! I see it not so.

Do these self-appointed language-police really think that the use of a cliché indicates that one doesn't apprehend what one writes? Hopefully, some of us actually read the words we lay down on the page (clichés included) and have determined that, as recorded, they rightfully belong there. Clichés can be to writing what formulas are to mathematics: short cuts of expression, Rosetta stones of communication, foils for other words and expressions. Though our eye is generally on the cue-ball, cushions are frequently required to execute a proper shot.

Unsung Heroes, my tribute to this linguistic persona non grata appears in the "Appendices," page ___.

close call — Even Peter Roget couldn't come up with a one word equivalent — so close call it is. In 1970, I designed and "helped" build a fairly elaborate home "back-in-the-woods" on forested acreage some fifty miles west of Minneapolis. I found the location because I owned a lake home in the vicinity, which was a great getaway with but a single major shortcoming, the unreliability of the electric power provider. Consequently, I outfitted the new home's attached garage with a fancy electric generator that ran on LP gas — which was also the furnace fuel. The generator had enough capacity to run about a dozen houses and drew the LP from my thousand-gallon tank situated down by the township road, some thousand feet distant.

My electrician cousin and I installed the home's electric wiring, complicated lighting system, intercom, and all the gadgetry necessary for a fully automatic power supply (excepting an every-other month, five-minute maintenance run of the generator motor). We paid particular and careful attention to installing the flexible, stainless steel exhaust tube that ran through a special insulating collar in the garage wall and attached to a muffler mounted outside.

A year went by and the automatic system performed flawlessly. Several outages occurred and, aside from a blink-of-the-eye flicker from illuminated light bulbs and the distant thrum from the generator motor, we hardly noticed.

However, a cold March morning "backdropped" a flaw. I awakened at 4:30 a.m. to frantic barking. Our three large dogs that slept in the back hall opening to the garage were normally rather quiet, and though I felt a little headachy and groggy (very unusual for me), their extraordinary behavior prompted me to check on them. Immediately apparent, pulsing noise from the generator motor filled the back stairs; opening the door to the back hallway was akin to standing alongside a small airfield. No wonder the dogs were acting crazy. However, opening the hallway door to the garage was like being dropped into a 1930s locomotive foundry, the palpable noise was overwhelming.

Throbbing explosions bounced from the bare wood and plasterboard walls and blue-white, smoky fumes filled the large garage.

The roiling gray torrent and deafening noise streamed from the end of the generator motor's exhaust tube, the end of which twitched crazily on the garage floor. Somehow, it had detached from both the mounting bracket and the outside muffler and worked its way inside. Ninety-nine times out of a hundred, the flexible exhaust line would have just hung down outside the garage and no problem ensued — however, this was that unlikely three-digit event.

I pulled the cutoff switch; the engine coughed and fell silent, the stainless steel snake stilled. I pushed a garage-door opener, forgetting there was now no electric power. Then, hurriedly, I pulled the manual release cord and heaved up a heavy door. The dogs raced outside and I returned upstairs to explain that the power would be off until I could fix the exhaust system. I reached the upper floor just in time to hear my wife call, "Hey, the water stopped." The pressure tank had provided initial shower water, but, with no power to run the pump, no further water. Nearly concurrent with her words, a large "thump" came from the shower room. "Why are you showering before I can get the lights back on?" I asked, as I passed the bathroom entrance, "What was that noise?" No answer. Irritated, as much from my headache as her silence, I again called from the bedroom. "What the devil was that?"

No response. And then, I thought, My God! Could it be possible? I rushed into the pitch-black bathroom, calling my wife's name several times, and pulled open the shower door. I could see absolutely nothing but heard a moan from the floor. Frantically, I felt around and touched JoAnn's hand. Grasping it and pulling, I tried to lift her to her feet. She moaned again but remained completely unresponsive. My strength seemed strangely sapped and I struggled to lift her up, but she was wet and slippery and as dead a weight as a sack of flour. Getting a grip beneath her arms, I dragged her along the hallway to a small, shoulder-high, crank-out window. Ironically, when I was designing the house, it was a window she had argued against, wanting that entire wall for some family photos. Luckily for her, natural light in the hallway trumped photographs. As I cranked open the disputed window, she came half awake and struggled to free herself from my grip. "Leggo," she mumbled, then twisted and screamed, "leggo!" She was still slippery and it consumed all my strength to keep her gyrating body erect enough to keep her head by the tiny source of fresh air.

By that time, I realized the cause of her behavior; at least I thought I did. Years before, when at the University, I attended a party where a backyard charcoal grill was moved indoors because of unanticipated rain. An hour or so later, there were a couple of kids semi passed out and acting crazy, like JoAnn was now, and the rest of us had first-class headaches—carbon monoxide is tough stuff. Still, how could that silent killer get through well sealed, double-thick garage walls and make its way up to our second floor?

And then it struck me like a sledgehammer. Susan's bedroom abutted the garage; where the hell was Susan?

"Susan!" I screamed. "Wake up! Get up here!"

No reply.

"Susan! Susan!" I bellowed loud enough to be heard in Annandale, five miles distant.

A faint, "Yes, Daddy . . . head hurts." Thank God! She was alive.

I dared not release JoAnn. She showed no signs of awareness and I wasn't sure I had enough strength left to go down, get Susan, and fight JoAnn's body upright again. So, I screamed, "Come on, Sweetheart, come upstairs!"

I listened, which was difficult as my wife's thrashing and babbling prevented hearing any small sounds.

"Suzy! Get the hell upstairs!" Again, JoAnn involuntarily winced at my scream. "Shut up," she said. But that was better than no response.

"Hey, Susan . . . Please . . . come . . ." My voice broke, vocal cords strained past vibrating.

"I'm . . . coming . . . coming, Daddy," my daughter's voice came from the bottom of the stairs.

"Oh, Suzy, Suzy, get up here," I managed to croak.

I suppose it was but a matter of seconds, though it seemed like hours, when I realized Susan had not joined us. Again, I barely managed to get out a few words: "Suze, you there?"

"Yeah . . . yeah, I'm coming."

Thankfully, JoAnn had lapsed into silence and I could hear Susan. She must have pulled herself upright by grasping the stair railing. I heard a small sound, somewhat resembling a slap, and then, though I managed to gasp out a call several times, Susan did not reply. I guess she must have fainted and hit her head on the sharp-edged wood banister. Whatever had happened, she finally crawled to the stair top with a scalp laceration nearly three inches long, right down to the bone. It bled profusely.

Another hour and JoAnn had regained her senses, Susan's head was bound with one of my T-shirts, the house mostly cleared of noxiousness, the dogs fed and relaxed and Susan and I were headed into Buffalo to the doctors. I cautioned Susan against relating our long story of survival and suggested that she just tell the doctor the exact, but less complicated truth, that she fell on the stairs. Some two hours, twenty-five stitches, sour looks and not-so-subtle-intimations-of-child-abuse from doctor and staff later, we all gathered around the breakfast table and rehashed our ordeal. The dogs were invited into the kitchen for treats and extra dog food. After all, I think anyone saving your life is entitled to all the dog food they can eat.

commodious—I love the English language, as used in the US; it's kept me on my semantic toes for eight decades. Like my own sweet country, it embraces newcomers, barely tolerates the elderly (many useful words are sent to the archaic poor-farm), often favoring zingy new models, and as a communicative tool, it ranks right up there with the pyramids as a world wonder. Example: On the way to view our present home, the real estate saleswoman opined that, "You'll just love this place, it's so commodious!" To this day, I'm not sure if she referred to the spacious layout or the four bathrooms.

C.U.Lex—The pen name used for *From the Lowlands*, my ephemeral, "humorous" newspaper column. No one, that I am aware of, ever recognized the significance of the pseudonym. It just couldn't be that my pen name, like my humor, is a little obscure? Naaah.

D

dancing — as an art form, I think it ranks somewhere between bank robbery and Ping-Pong. Of course, that's just the opinion of a man with two left feet — and if you think dancing shoes are expensive, you should try buying two, size nine, patent leather lefties!

darn fool — until I was about twelve, I thought this was my name. Thanks Dad.

debt — I'm pretty tough on my father in these pages. Lacking the character to "forgive and forget," I've "gotten even" with Dad by exposing some of his (as I perceived them) parental deficiencies. Nonetheless, rudimentary fairness directs me to outline the debt that I owe him for providing a safe, if not nurturing, home, a sense of stability, English-model ethics (such as paying one's debts, convenient or not) and not a few negative examples, which have served me well. For this, thank you, Dad. The debt I can never discharge is your gift of exposing me to classical music; this more than balances the scales of our contentious relationship, in your favor.

dedication — Instead of treating this word as a noun, I'll make it a proper noun: Finley McMartin.

To others, I believe that my Uncle Finley was a remarkably unremarkable man. To me, he was a remarkably remarkable man. I could have listed him under many superlatives, but dedication seems inclusive of faith, constancy, duty and selflessness. Quiet, temperate, mild of manner when he spoke, he must have seemed to most very bland and uninteresting. I cannot recall ever hearing him express an opinion (outside of Sunday school) and remember but two occasions when he raised his soft, gravely voice in anger, both engendered by me. However, I will not relate those instances here. I'll recount a little of what I saw, heard, and overheard that makes him such a hero in my eyes. I'll also add that my inferences are, of course, of questionable accuracy.

When I was a boy of five or six, Uncle Finley was in his seventies and the few events in his earlier life, which he recounted to me, seemed like tales from ancient dark ages. He was the eldest of nine or ten children and at about age eleven, on the death of his mother in childbirth, he permanently withdrew from school to care for the family brood. His lack of formal schooling notwithstanding, the scope of his self-taught education was considerable, demonstrable by long-time stints as County Assessor and the Sunday School Superintendent of the Claremont Presbyterian church.

Once he recalled that when he was a boy, a "pike" as long as he was tall, was taken from the creek that ran through his farm. (The creek was a fork of the Zumbro river which eventually empties into the Mississippi). Another night, while carrying home a ham from a neighbor's house, he was followed by a snarling, chuffing beast. In the morning, some older men identified the beast's tracks as a mountain lion. It surely was the ancient dark ages. What the reader must understand is that Uncle Finley would have rather lain on the Claremont railroad tracks than lie about or exaggerate his experiences.

As a young man, late teens or early twenties, he jumped from a haymow and, as a result, developed what he described as "a rheumatism" in his hips and legs, causing him to walk with a slight but painful limp. Following his hurtful leap, he never again enjoyed a nighttime rest free of pain. As long as I knew them, he and Aunt Katherine kept separate bedrooms, ostensibly due to Uncle Finley's nocturnal thrashing. The rest of the family clandestinely smirked about the arrangement.

Married late in life, Aunt Katherine was a fanatical Christian, and it was assumed by all that she was a stranger to copulation, but Finley's pain was genuine and they simply accommodated to it. How would I, a six year old, know anything about my zealous Aunt's attitude toward sex, when she would rather have been caged with rats than even speak the word? That is a story recounted herein; see **fishing**.

Speed is a relative concept. In those early years in Claremont, I thought giddy speed was a ride in Uncle Finley's buggy, behind the gyrating hindquarters of one brown and one black horse. It was more than half a mile uptown and for whatever purpose—a trip to Jack Rand's hardware, Skinny Springstead's grocery store, or the lumberyard—Nance and Bess would have to be outfitted with heavy, cumbersome harnesses and hitched to the buggy. I loved those occasions and could hardly wait to make the trips. I was thrilled and felt very important when permitted to hold the reins and drive the team. Actually, Nance and Bess knew exactly where to go and at what pace they would use to get there. A buggy-whip stood in its tube-like holder, but it was strictly decorative, at least I never saw it used as anything but a tool to knock clay from the big, thin buggy wheels. Uncle Finley controlled our speed with a few clucks of the tongue or a low "easy, easy." It didn't take a psychologist, or even a small boy, to see that Uncle Finley loved his horses.

His regard for his team manifested in many ways. First off, he gave them a rest on Sundays. And, though he must have been in pain as he hobbled the half-mile to church each Sunday, I don't believe he missed a single week in fifty years. Cars had replaced most horse drawn vehicles by then, but I do remember an occasional buggy and team tethered to the rail in front of the church. However, as Uncle Finley led the Sunday school in one of his favorite hymns like *In the Garden* or *The Old Rugged Cross*, Nance and Bess were contentedly munching hay in their stalls.

This will be germane to Uncle Finley's love for his horses—trust me. I think my paternal grandfather was pretty great. He was a dynamo, quite unlike Uncle Finley. The two men lived with but a single house separating their homes and married very close sisters. Their lives intertwined more closely than, perhaps, either wished. During my Claremont days, Minnesota levied a tax on personal property. Uncle Finley knew of every purchase made by Grandpa, and as County Assessor, scrupulously applied the personal property tax on every penny of both his own and Grandpa's property. The difference was that Uncle Finley didn't have much and Grandpa had quite a bit. My grandfather owned the first rubber-tired tractor in Dodge County (when everyone else laughed and said the damn contraption would never get through mud) and the first two combines. He worked harder than any other two men put together that I have ever known. He knew full well that some other farmer would have just pulled one of those combines into his machine shed and "forgotten" to tell the assessor. Of course, Uncle Finley naively accepted what was reported. Grandpa chafed at the unfairness, but reserved his greatest contempt for the trees in his brother-in-law's field.

When most were farming with tractors, Uncle Finley still used his team to plow, plant, and harvest. He scratched out a living on sixty acres of black, Dodge County soil and dressed it regularly with a mixture of horse manure and straw. No fence surrounded the land that lay about a mile straight south of town. However, the entry road was fronted by a rusting, opened gate, overgrown with years of grass, vines and brush. That was Uncle Finley, absolutely open, no defenses. Surrogates for Uncle Finley, the objects of Grandpa's scorn were half a dozen or so mature oaks scattered throughout the acreage. "No farmer worth his salt would ever let trees grow in his field!" Both men had died before I realized that my Grandfather never knew the purpose of Uncle Finley's trees; I thought it not at all unusual, as I played by the creek, to see Uncle Finley resting his horses beneath the green canopies. Many times he sat in the sun on whatever implement he was using, while the horses cooled in the shade. I suppose it was just too painful for him to get off, hobble to the shadows, and limp back to the iron seat. I interpret that as true concern for your horses.

When Nance and Bess aged passed their ability to work, Uncle Finley retired. He sold the farm to my father who promptly had the trees bulldozed and burned. Nance and Bess lived out their years on the two or three acre plot by the barn; when the last of the two died, Uncle Finley sold the house and grounds and put himself into the County Home—not a tax supported institution, but a private "old folks home" paid for by its residents. He lived out his days in a tiny room with a roommate that chewed tobacco and constantly spit in, or close to, a brass spittoon. On my last visit, Uncle Finley said he wished only to see his maker "as soon as possible." I try to recall this gentle, kindly man in less dour circumstances.

For instance, though Uncle Finley kept up with current events via radio (his single extravagance) and the weekly newspaper (if one might dignify the Claremont News as such), he preferred many of the familiar amenities of his youth. For example, though his house stood within the village of Claremont, albeit with a barn and a two or three acre pasture, it was a good length of time after settling in the home before indoor plumbing was installed. Avoiding the new-fangled flush toilet, he continued to use the outhouse, situated midway between the house and the barn.

Though outhouses were fairly common during my Claremont years, those who had the luxury of indoor plumbing generally used it. This predilection of Uncle Finley's was regarded as peculiar and not overlooked by the town's teens, particularly at Halloween. (And you must realize that in our town of four hundred souls, one's most personal habits were often the subject of popular speculation and judgment, especially judgment.) Each year, as regularly as the drought of the Depression years produced a stunted harvest, fun-loving Claremont youth tipped over Uncle Finley's outhouse.

I recall more than once, on the day after Halloween, the moon on the outhouse door rising to its rightful position in the Claremont firmament, easy work for Nance and Bess as they pulled on ropes attached to the small wooden structure. And, after my Uncle nailed a few patches in place, the little building was as functional as ever.

I was in the third grade during my last year in Claremont, old enough to appreciate my Uncle's riposte to the town's Halloween hooligans. I don't think his idea was original, possibly gleaned from *The Country Gentleman* or *Capper's Farmer*. His outhouse was nestled between a decorous screen of lilacs, but open to both front and rear (no pun intended) and was occasionally moved forward or backward over a fresh excavation, as the distance to the top of the pit's contents rose with use.

On my last Halloween in Claremont, peculiar old Finley McMartin created quite a stir. It seemed that two of Claremont's young swains had "needed a bathroom break" and McMartin's outhouse was close at hand—never mind that it was during a pitch black Halloween night—and that McMartin had carelessly and maliciously moved his outhouse, creating an unwarranted danger to persons needing natural relief and resulting in the immersion of aforesaid youths in foul and malodorous offal. My Uncle explained: "Got to move an outhouse once in a while, just didn't have the time to get the lime in and fill the hole." No one thought to notice that no new hole had been dug. I think the sheriff even inquired if Uncle Finley wanted to file a trespass notice.

Uncle Finley declined to press trespassing charges, which in those days, would have probably stuck. My guess is that he was satisfied with what got stuck on the Halloween vandals.

Dingo — As a preschool child, I never tired of Rudyard Kipling's *Just So Stories*. It must have driven my Grandmother to the brink of despair at my ten thousandth importunity to "read Yellow Dog Dingo." I cringe at my recollection of demanding, "Read, read." What a brat! She should have taken a cue from Kipling's Gunga Din and done a little belting and flaying, but she was too patient and loving; she would simply read; perhaps she eventually recited it from memory. I do not know why I fixated on such a tangential Kipling character, but for me, Yellow Dog Dingo's chase was more arresting than "How the Rhinoceros Got his Skin" or the giraffe's acquisition of a long neck. Therefore, when presented with a mewling, fury yellow ball, its name was not an option; Dingo had jumped from Kipling's page, right into my lap.

I think I was pushing five years old when Dingo came to live with us. We had moved from Grandpa's to the Weber house (I think the owner, Mr. Weber, was a country dwelling farmer). Dad had been elected Mayor of Claremont, and received a salary of twenty dollars a month, which, coincidently, was precisely our monthly rent. I was heartbroken to leave (even by a half-mile) the loving proximity of my paternal grandmother. Even then, I could sense the growing estrangement between my parents and me. Dingo was loving warmth in a frigid home, literally. He was strictly an outside dog (as most were in those days), but when I could, I sneaked him to my bedroom on the second floor. It was ostensibly "heated" via an ornamental cast iron grill set into the floor over the dining room below. The first floor received heat through a similar, but larger, grill in the center of the dining room floor. The furnace hunkered in an earthen pit below the dining room. I remember feeling so very fortunate on those cold, rare nights when Dingo kept me warm and kept me company.

There was no running water in the house, other than a hand-pump at one end of the kitchen sink, and Mother thoughtfully provided me a hand-bowl type pan of water in my bedroom, to what purpose, I am still unaware. However, I used it as drinking water for Dingo, though sometimes I had to break a scab of ice for him. Noticing the nearly empty pan one day, Mom asked what I needed water for; evidently, its purpose evaded her, too.

I am a living cliché of the countless boy-and-his-dog stories. Dingo was my playmate, confidant, fishing buddy, best friend, and sometimes a surrogate victim of my father's anger toward me. I loved him as a brother, and though I'm sure he reciprocated, he was, nonetheless, an independent creature. I remember some very hot summer days when I trudged all over Claremont calling him, asking anyone I met (and everyone in Claremont knew both of us well) if they'd seen Dingo. On more than one fruitless search, I remember the pain swelling in my throat. I recall dejectedly turning into the back yard, there greeted by my enormous furry friend, crawling from the low, cool, cave-like space beneath the back porch. With a yawn and luxurious stretch, front legs extended in a sort of low bow, he'd wag his tail as if he'd been with me all day; I don't suppose he ever understood why I hugged him so tightly and cried like a baby. I will never understand why his cool hideaway wasn't the first place to search for him. Dad wasn't all wrong about "stupid."

His troglodyte act notwithstanding, Dingo was loyal and caring. Each day he accompanied me on the block-long walk to school, and when we reached the playground—the small grassless area girdling the schoolhouse—he would turn and trot back toward home. The first and second grade classroom overlooked one of Claremont's few sidewalks and the Presbyterian Church. Our teacher, Miss Casey, never concealed her delight when, each school-day, just a minute or so before the noon siren blew, Dingo would appear on the sidewalk, waiting to escort me home. One day, after observing Dingo waiting for several minutes, Miss Casey said, "I guess we can go to lunch now, class, Dingo says it's noon." Later, we learned that the town siren's electrical switch had malfunctioned, the problem was both diagnosed and remedied by the Mayor (Dad could change a switch as he was a graduate electrical engineer).

Dingo was as friendly as he was large, over a hundred pounds worth of licking, hair-shedding, tail-wagging, friendly. And, until the very end, his few episodes of savagery (defined by today's standards) were simply ignored.

Depression era lip-service to social decorum demanded much contravention to reality. All brides were virgin, husbands faithful, church goers' sin free, and dogs submissive at all times. I knew folks who kept quite vicious dogs, so intimidating that one would never dream of walking past their owners' premises. Dingo, however, presented an unusually friendly persona to everyone—almost. The milkman and the Catholic priest's yappy little Boston bull terrier were long-running exceptions, but otherwise, I observed but a single lapse in my dog's placid disposition. And then, just possibly, Dingo acted on an understanding greatly surpassing his human's.

Mother made wonderful macaroni and cheese in a deep, finely decorated dish purchased from the Jewel Tea Man. How she managed to maneuver my father into unsnapping his purse for such a borderline frivolity is a mystery. Perhaps she emulated Lysistrata, or perhaps Dad favored the rare, tasty diversion from fried apples and other equally noxious Depression fare, for he seemed quite happy with the transaction.

The purveyor of pots, pans and pretty dishes evidently shared the happiness, as he made us a regular stop on his visits to Claremont. Not once, in at least a dozen visits, did Dingo pay him attention beyond a cursory sniff and a "hello" tail-wag. The Jewel Tea Man's final call came on a warm, autumn day. I was helping Dad nail tarpaper around the foundation, which was an annual chore to reduce wintry drafts. We were working at the side of the house, but paused to watch the itinerate salesman stagger beneath an amazingly large load of samples. Dingo greeted him enthusiastically, prancing in circles as the man walked by us as on the way to the back porch. After his customary, friendly welcome, Dingo usually ignored the fellow. This day, however, as Mr. Jewel Tea approached the back porch, Dingo made a mighty leap to the porch (no more than a roofed platform raised a foot and a half from the ground), turned toward the incredulous peddler and, showing about a bushel basket's worth of teeth, snarled so viciously that the frightened fellow's armload of pots and utensils clattered to the ground.

My father, an equal dispenser of discipline to son or dog, had only to point and stare at Dingo. His glare, predating destructive lasers by nearly thirty years, was all that was necessary to transmute the vicious beast that slavered on our back porch to friendly mutt.

"It's okay now . . ."

As the shaken Jewel Tea man began picking up his scattered wares, Dad continued, "Go on, he'll be fine."

It was true. Dingo hopped from the stoop, wagged his tail, and, after sniffing at the frightened man's ankle, crawled under the porch.

I felt embarrassed for Dingo, who knew fear in no other circumstance, but cowered before my father. However, I knew the feeling, intimately; it's called saving one's backside. We never saw The Jewel Tea Man again. A few weeks later Claremont gossip featured that very peddler—something about removing property from customers' homes. I no longer ask myself what did Dingo know; I now ask, how did Dingo know?

These recitals of Dingo's "misbehavior" need context because social mores have undergone evolutions unimagined in the rural environment of my childhood. In the Depression thirties, the majority of dogs were not conscientiously accorded warmth, dry shelter, medical care, or even sympathy. In agrarian Claremont, shooting an injured dog could be considered superfluous sympathy and veterinary care generally meant dispensing potions to horses with the dry-heaves or inserting an arm into the backside cavity of a pregnant heifer. Paid medical interventions for an ailing dog or cat would have been considered outrageous.

However, unless the attack was egregious, a person bitten by a dog was expected to buck up and keep their mouth shut, though I knew of a couple of dog owners who voluntarily paid a victim's medical bills—perhaps two or three dollars. This indifference to dog attacks was a somewhat institutionalized attitude. I believe Minnesota law gave dogs the first bite free, that is, only after a second attack was a dog officially deemed "vicious."

Therefore, Dingo's aggression against Dean Hyland, the milkman, was not unusual or alarming. Dean's family lived on the edge of town and provided the town's commercial milk supply. His defense (and he had plenty of practice) against combative dogs, a long, stout walking stick, discouraged the most belligerent canines. Dingo did his best to intimidate Dean, but the daily outcome was the same: Milkman's stick, 1; Dingo, 0. We surmised that Dean had used his walking stick too freely when Dingo was a puppy, thus incurring the dog's lasting hatred.

I believe that dogs absorb the attitudes of their owners, but possibly manifest those attitudes in canine fashion, how else to explain Dingo's antipathy to the priest's terrier. Claremont seethed with small dogs, none of which incurred the slightest notice from my dog, even if they attempted to nip him. On Claremont's Presbyterian east side, Catholics, and especially the town's priest, were viewed and invariably referred to, in contemptible, déclassé terms, or worse. They were the last to settle the community: bad. Most were Polish: worse. And, horrors, they "took orders from the Pope." What more could one wish for in a social pariah? Of course, I had no notion of how the West-enders viewed us snooty Presbyterians. The priest's feisty little Boston bull, seemingly devoid of fear or common sense, deliberately attacked Dingo, whenever the two were in proximity. (Could that puny beast possibly have acquired resentment, of we superior folk and our canine surrogates, from his humans?) Their confrontations might happen anywhere, but on summer Saturday nights, when the bandstand was hung with a sheet for the merchants' presentation of a Felix the Cat movie, or a silent Rudolph Valentino, the two dogs were sure to find each other.

Their collisions were formulaically loud and brief. Backdropped by a whirlwind of ferocious, guttural snarling, the Boston bull would make an ineffective dive for Dingo's front leg. Dingo would seize the diminutive, shorthaired inferno by the back, shake the daylights out of him, and deposit the helplessly dizzy little fellow on the ground, no worse for the experience than scratches. The priest would snatch up his disoriented pet and the ring of onlookers would drift away. The Presbyterians shook their heads, nodding to each other with a what-else-could-you-expect-from-a-priest's-dog look. The country dwelling German Lutherans laughed heartily, while folks from the West side of town looked grim.

I would not learn of Dingo's final bout with his canine adversary until more than a dozen years after the fact.

Last Words: Frederick's Bionary

Miss Casey, my second grade teacher, noticed Dingo's absence almost as soon as I. Green leaves struggled to escape their husks and robins had already begun to trowel mud into sturdy nurseries, but Dingo no longer kept his noontime appointments. When she inquired, I burst into tears. He had been missing for nearly a week. I had patrolled every house and yard, every vacant lot, every ditch and dump, canvassing the length and breadth of Claremont more than a dozen times and called until my voice failed. I had even braved the spiders beneath the back porch in my futile search. I remember the frightful pain in my throat, the palpable sensation of emptiness in my chest, and even worse, a vague dread that I would never find my beloved friend again. A family member, I can't remember who, suggested that he "ran away," a not unheard of circumstance for dogs in those days. Nothing, however, assuaged my sorrow. Eventually, I accepted my friend's absence and still later, Dingo was just another memory, albeit precious.

My grandfather's death was the first in my immediate family and, though I was a junior in University, the first open casket funeral I attended; to this day I have a very clear picture of him at the last viewing. I have such clear recollections of much of my early life and, therefore, am perplexed that I have no memories of the circumstances that led to a rare, serious conversation with my mother following Grandfather's funeral. I do remember the shocker, as if she were at my side right now.

I had made an appreciative comment to the effect that Grandpa had fostered my love of animals, never failing to pick up a turtle on the road or stop his tractor and gather up an owl, baby gopher, or whatever, and bring them to me. Mother, who was acutely sensitive to our less than cordial relationship, but made no effort to improve it, might have felt that I made a disparaging comparison and said, "He wasn't always so wonderful, you know."

"What do you mean by that?"

"It's time you knew about Dingo," she said.

She had my attention. "And . . ."

She related the long held family secret. Dingo had followed my Grandfather into Claremont's off-and-on McCall's Drug Store. There, they encountered the priest and his dog. The inevitable ensued, causing significant damage, for which Grandfather paid, on the spot. He also purchased chloroform and put Dingo down, right there in the drug store.

Many boy-and-his-dog stories end happily or heroically; this one is an exception.

director — I have worn the Director's title a number of times. I was the Executive Director of Chamber Music Minnesota for fifteen years (its entire existence) where I produced Music da Camera, a television program of chamber music — available to some twenty million American homes and ultimately, through Voice of America telecasts, another hundred million or so around the world. I have also served on a dozen or so governing boards, foundations and commissions as a director.

distance — In my experience, most folks don't lose much sleep contemplating the philosophical nuances of the word, distance; they're content to say, "It's a couple of miles to the shopping center." On the other hand, word-geeks (mea culpa) and poets (e.g. John Donne) seem not to share the common indifference to the word. My slightly out-of-date Webster's offers several definitions, two, especially thought provoking to me. The first is, "The extent of space between points on a linearly measured course;" its particular relevance to me is the approximately two hundred fifty miles between my hometown of Claremont, Minnesota, and Virginia, Minnesota — hometown of second wife, JoAnn.

The first time I accompanied my spouse-to-be, to her iron-range home, I experienced minor culture shock. Not only did her ancestral dwelling teeter on the brink of the vast Mesabi open iron mine pit, not so muffled explosions rumbled with jarring frequency — though the local folks didn't seem to notice the routine shakings. JoAnn explained that, as the mine expanded, by virtue of eminent domain, houses and streets were simply ripped away to accommodate the ever-enlarging void. We entered her childhood home through a side door, directly into the kitchen. A round, white oilcloth covered table held large salt and peppershakers, and a couple of partially consumed bottles of whisky. It contrasted with a similar table in my grandmother's home except that, there, the white oilcloth invariably backgrounded a plate of raspberry tarts — rings of

Rocky

cinnamon sprinkled piecrust filled with homemade black raspberry jam.

    This is not a brief against alcohol. On that first visit to Virginia, I enjoyed several social calls to JoAnn's friend's homes, and consumed not a few libations poured from liquor bottles billeted on kitchen tabletops. However, the kitchen tables in the homes of my Grandmother, where I spent formative years, and JoAnn's home in Virginia, proved to be an unfortunate metaphor of relationship. During nearly thirty years of marriage, physical space between us, whether calculated in miles or millimeters, posed no difficulty. Yet, the gulf-like distance between those kitchen table settings proved unbridgeable.

Were nearly three decades enough time to learn anything about distance? I'm not sure. One can usually effect a change in linear distance to a fixed place. Not so easy is an answer to another of Webster's pithy and thought provoking definitions of distance: "The degree of deviation or difference that separates two things in relationship" — particularly if the "two things" are people, and the "difference" is a whisky bottle and a plate of tarts.

dog — I love dogs. Some of my best friends have been dogs. Like Rocky, a German shepherd, who joined our family at about six months of age because his owner no longer wanted him. He was panicked when I picked him up from his confinement in a warehouse where his previous owner roughly corralled him with a rope. It took all my strength to get him into the front seat of the pickup. When we got home, I sat him in a circle with Watson, Goldie, Winkie (his to-be canine siblings) and me. I still marvel that the other dogs seemed to understand as they patiently sat and listened for three hours as I assured Rocky that he'd found a good home where there would be plenty of food and love. Finally, I took a chance and released the rope. Far from bolting, he moved to my side. It was difficult not to think of him as Dingo reincarnated. However, he was distinctly a unique personality. I was lucky enough to photograph him sitting in the snow, a picture that appeared on numerous phone book covers. As he reached his prime, he was shot by an unknown neighbor, the circumstances of which, I do not know. He lived, in pain, for another six months.

When Rocky said Goodbye

> Rocky came and sat
> Beside my chair.
> He sat as straight

As recent surgery
And pain permitted.
With a solemn, gentle thrust,
He pushed his nose upon my lap.
I laid my pen aside
And scratched his ears;
I fought to match his dignity,
I fought to check my tears.
I stroked his velvet muzzle;
His nose was dry and fevered.
His eyes, soft caramel pools,
Seemed bent on telling me
The jaw of memory would tightly grip
This moment shared
Between a dog and man,
Memory that blurs . . . distinctions.
Memory: inescapable, interminable leash.
Next spring, I know that he will pad
In spectral step,
Along the forest path with me,
In search for fresh-sprung flowers.
And he will wait, cool, with endless patience,
In a pool of shade cast by a friendly oak,
As I perspire and coax
The angry August bees
To share their summer store.
And, when next I battle winter's ivory siege
With sweat and shovel,
He, most likely,
Will be taking ghostly ease
Atop a nearby drift,
Steadfast,
Waiting on my whim
To call him to my side.
As now he waits the last command,
In calm forbearance,
Accepting this, the awful thing

Frederick Blanch

Rocky and author

That is his final master . . .
The thing that is my master too.
Would that I shall muster
His serenity, by half,

When my turn comes. If so,
I shall be more a man than I am now.
Although, I am a wiser man
For having looked within his faded eye
And seen that what has been for us,
Will always be, for memory
Will loath to let this friendship end.

Yet,
I shall be a man diminished . . .
When I have lost my friend.

door — There are doors and then there are doors, from massive bulwarks like the Great Gates of Kiev, which inspire poetry, music, and awe, to tiny portals closeting time-keeping cuckoos, inspiring little more than a confirming glance at one's watch. Ubiquitous of purpose, doors may open to unimagined educational vistas, or, as easily, conceal ladies or tigers, or, as in my case, a sister.

During the final months of my mother's second pregnancy, I contracted whooping cough and lived with my grandparents. I was also forbidden entry to first grade through September. School officials suggested I stay out the entire year, had Grandma not been President of the Claremont School Board, my education might have suffered a year's delay. However, a couple of weeks following the start of classes, Grandmother marched me into school and, as best I can recall, no mass extinctions resulted. I do recall that a few days later Dad was stuck with picking me up from school and that we left from there to pick up Mom and my newborn sibling from the hospital in Owatonna. On the thirteen-mile drive home, Mother sat in the back seat with baby Priscilla, but still couldn't avoid my nonstop barrage of questions. Dad drove tightlipped, looking like he might limber up his swatting arm at any moment, but curiosity overwhelmed my fear. Mom hedged and dodged, but somehow, I wheedled the information that she didn't actually find my sister in a hallway at the hospital. "Where was she, then?" I importuned.

"She grew inside my body."

"How did she get out?" I asked skeptically.

"Through a little door under my heart."

"Oh, gee! I wanna see it! . . . I wanna see it!"

Dad abruptly slammed the door on further physiological education with a preemptory, "Shut up!"

Thus, for a few years, that door remained closed.

E

ego — Like many folks, I was endowed with one of these. Truth and modesty prevent me from estimating its extent; I can't describe it with accuracy because, despite assiduous efforts, I've never managed to make the journey completely around mine.

employment — In 1940 the country seemed drifting back into economic depression. Nonetheless, most grown men turned up their noses at an arduous job paying but one dollar a day — a long, ten plus hour day — which created an opportunity for me to apply for my first job. Two years before, Dad had accepted a job requiring us to move to the city. However, to my parent's relief, I spent summers in Claremont with my grandparents.

A tenant, Mr. Christy, had moved into Mr. Malik's farm (just across the gravel road behind Grandpa's place) and needed help to get a hay-crop into the barn. At that time, hay was cut by a machine called a side-delivery, which left the hay lying on the ground in long rows; muscle-power was required to wield long-handled, three or four tined forks and pitch large wads of hay onto a wagon as it was pulled up and down the field between the rows of fodder. And, in spite of its use as a prop for Grant Wood and Hollywood movies about peasants in revolt, I wouldn't be surprised if the word pitchfork originated from the implement's use as a tool for pitching hay.

The "help-wanted notice" had been distributed through normal channels, the gossip grapevine, and at the appointed time, about a dozen mostly teenaged "applicants" showed up in the barnyard to "interview" for the two-day job. Mr. Christy shook hands with four of our number promising: "Uh dollar uh day, if ya gimme an honest day's work." The contract was executed by a nod of the head, though one new employee did respond in a sotto voiced, "Don't work no other way." Most of the non-qualifiers shuffled off, but I, pretty much ignored during the whole process, spoke up.

"I can work as good as any uh these guys," I asserted.

My potential employer doffed his greasy cap, swiped a sweating forehead with a sleeve, and, shading his eyes with the cap's bill, squinted toward me. "You don't look like ya oughta even be here. How the heck old are ya?"

"Eleven." I didn't mention that I'd blown out eleven candles but two weeks earlier.

Mr. Christy smiled as he assessed my skinny, four-foot-six, seventy-five pound frame . "You ain't got much meat on ya, boy . . . I doubt ya could make it tah the noon whistle."

"Just try me . . . please!"

I think back and imagine he thought, "Oh damn! What now?"

"Please" was a sparingly used civility, not easily ignored. Plainly perplexed, he scratched at the graying stubble on his chin. No one else had actually talked about the job. And here was this damn runt of a kid making trouble. He looked away from me and gazed at the others; they were guys who understood that young punks didn't challenge the decisions of their elders. However, his face relaxed as his eye settled on Darrel Allen. When I still lived in Claremont, Darrel had been a classmate through second grade. When I went on to third grade, Darrel had been held back and, though academically retarded, his body had accelerated to the point that, when called on by Mr. Chtisty, he might easily have been confused with a high school senior. I remembered him as a bit of a bully, but, even though he lived on the Polish Catholic end of Claremont, he had never bothered me.

Totally ignoring Darrel, Mr. Christy said, "You fight Darrel, here, an' I'll see what kinda job ya can do." He didn't wait for my reply. "Take 'im on, Darrel."

I wanted to say "nothing doing." I almost bolted. Darrel would have easily made two of me, and his smirk suggested that he was going to enjoy a sanctioned opportunity to teach a mouthy little city slicker some respect. However, my feet were rooted to the ground, and a beating seemed preferable to the shame that would be forever attached to me if I ran. I would never dare show my face in Claremont again. I couldn't stand the thought that I might never see Grandma or Aunt Katherine again.

At that moment, any kind of thought was short-lived as Darrel grabbed me by the shoulders and hurled me down. It should have hurt, but I don't recall feeling much of anything, not even fear. My mouth got me into my predicament, but the rest of me seemed to know that it would have to do the extricating. Darrel pounced and proceeded to sit on my stomach, pinning my arms with hands the size of bushel baskets. My breathing nearly stopped, and out of reflex, I wrapped my legs around his waist and desperately tried to twist him sideways. He responded by standing, my legs still clutched him about his middle, and he spun like a top in an effort to shake me off. I remember spinning around and around and feeling very dizzy just before things turned black. Concurrently, I became aware of clamorous voices and yelling and that the fellows who had formed a loose ring about us were shouting encouragement . . . to me. I distinctly heard a "Hang in there, Sonny" (my Claremont nickname) and a "Jeezzzus Christ! The kid's uh . . ." I never heard what kind of "uh" the kid was, for my next conscious memory was of people fumbling with my feet. Darrel was sitting on the ground, my legs still tightly locked about his body. He was brushing chicken droppings and feathers from his shirtsleeve. Several hands were brushing the same materials from the back of my shirt. Darrel stuck out his hand and said, "No hard feelings."

"Naw," I answered. Actually, I had very little feeling of any kind. Though I told no one, I was numb for a week.

"Ya pitch hay like ya fight, you'll be okay." Mr. Christy was stuck with hiring me, but his prediction was spot on, and, though I pitched hay for the next two days, it was excruciating. Only the shame factor prevented me from quitting long before the noon whistle.

entomologist—As a boy, I thought I might grow up to be one of these. This was reinforced during my adolescence when quite a few young ladies referred to me as an entomologist, though they generally preferred a short interpolation of the word: insect.

entrepreneur—I must have inherited the spirit from my paternal grandfather as no other recent antecedent, to my knowledge, had much get-up-and-go. At the apogee of my business activity, I headed up half a dozen fairly successful enterprises.

F

father figure — The amount I would have paid to leave home and get away from my father.

firefighter — I spent the summer of 1945 with a large group of murderers, bank robbers, and assorted other miscreants; we fought forest fires together in the Klamath National Forest. During the Horse Creek Fire, one of them, a bulldozer driver, pushed through a wall of flame to extricate three trapped "tender-foot" firefighters; I was one of the rescued.

fishing — I've previously mentioned "the creek" (an obscure fork of the Zumbro river), a favorite haunt of my childhood. During the spring melt, it often overflowed its banks and flooded low places for several hundred yards on both sides. At all other times it was a benign trickle supporting a population of bullheads, suckers, and red horse; with a good running start, there were many places where it could be jumped without getting seriously wet — until beavers moved in. A scattering of oak, cherry, box-elder and huge elms and cottonwoods extended out for a half mile or so along both banks and generally served as pasturage for livestock; it also sheltered horned owls, hawks, foxes, woodchucks, an occasional badger, and hoards of crows whose main preoccupation seemed to be harassing the owls. It was paradise for a small boy who loved the outdoors, fascinated by the furred, feathered, insecta and amphibian inhabitants that abounded in an area generally ignored by adults.

Basically, the creek ran east and west, a shade more than a mile south of town. I thought nothing of the walk, even when loaded up with bamboo fishing poles, knapsack, a couple of glass jars for collecting unlucky toads, butterflies or whatever, a beat-up World War I Army canteen, and a great lunch of fried chicken sandwiches made with home grown black raspberry jam, and little, mocca cakes, lovingly fixed by either my Aunt or Grandmother.

Did I neglect to mention the bait can? It and its mucose, squirming contents were the most essential part of a fishing expedition to the creek. I'll digress here to engage in a little pedantry on fishing worms. There are earthworms and then there are earthworms, referred to as angleworms when I was a kid. Anyway, digging in the garden for good fishing worms was fairly arduous, yielding bait with paltry, pallid gray bodies, and modest numbers. However, just a few turns of the pitchfork in the manure pile yielded scores of plump, pink, foot-long night crawlers. And, though Zumbro fish were finicky, they were suckers (no pun intended) for juicy, manure-fattened, night crawlers. Of course, I wouldn't have dreamed of fishing without them.

Night crawlers are the fulcrum on which this little yarn turns.

You may remember, if you are reading this account alphabetically, that under **dedication**, I promised to relate the status of my Aunt Katherine's maidenhood and how I believe my insight on the matter, at age six, was superior to the adults who whispered about it.

In an era where many women still wore social mores like their Victorian hats, isolated in a rural community of four hundred souls, where very few residents owned those new-fangled radio things, where the weekly newspaper's scoops consisted of neighbors visiting neighbors, gossip flourished as a vital social activity. Intra-familial, inter-familial, and extra-familial gossip abounded; of course, children were excluded — theoretically.

At an early age, I became a practiced skulker. How else could a small child in an extended household of adults keep up on current gossip? Skulking prowess, and the acute preoccupation of the subject by family, accounted for my knowledge of and interest in my Great Aunt's bedroom arrangements. (You may recall that she and my Uncle maintained separate bedrooms.)

Aunt Katherine had married in her forties to a man who had courted and lost her sister (my Grandmother) — sort of a Mozartian scenario. She shed religiosity, regularly, copiously, and noticeably, like dandruff on a dark suit. Dancing was a sin. Cursing was a sin. A deck of cards: the Devil's playthings. Strong drink was sinful as well as a litany of actions most folks consider ordinary living. Lust, oh, please, pardon the word, qualified as the most evil of forbidden topics. Should a reference to reproduction escape one's lips (which, in a farm community like Claremont, was very likely to occur), the heavens might open and St. Peter himself smite the guilty degenerate with the scepter of God. Though she was wonderful to me and I loved her dearly—and will till my last breath—I recognized her religious views as somewhat beyond the usual—like a million miles.

Therefore, on a sunlit spring day, as my dear Aunt and I dug for fishing worms in the manure pile next to the barn, I was privileged to glimpse her private (and completely unknown) attitude toward plain old sex. I pulled out an especially fat crawler that turned out to be two of the creatures joined in what might be described (in the Depression era) as a romantic embrace. I held them up for close examination and my aunt snatched them away and plopped them into the bait-can.

Somewhat nettled that my scientific curiosity had been unceremoniously stifled, and with all the authority of a worldly six-year-old, I said, "I know what they're doing."

Aunt Katherine hesitated not a moment but said, "Under the right circumstances, with God's blessing, that is the most pure and wonderful act in the world."

Uncharacteristically, I never breathed her words until long after her death and then, only to my mother; to this day, I regret that breech of trust.

The family continued to speculate on the import of two bedrooms and fished for hints wherever they could, but they were using the wrong bait; they should have used night crawlers.

G

Gemini — That's me: June 13, 1929. I don't believe in astrological hocus pocus, but that doesn't prove anything. I guess there's always been at least a couple of me. A little more conservative than I suppose Genghis Kan to be, I am, nonetheless, relatively unconventional. Is unconventional conservative an oxymoron? Dad used to say I was a moron. But as I remember, his modifying adjectives were always more colorful than unconventional.

generosity — If a role model for generosity facilitates its development, I should have become a regular cornucopia of philanthropy, mirroring my paternal grandfather. This story is but one of many examples of my grandfather's abruptly honest yet charitable nature, illustrating the power of deed compared to facile words.

It was an unseasonably warm evening in late April or early May, and after supper, my grandfather and I took advantage of the comfortable temperature to sit on the normally cold stone of the back steps. I cannot remember the story my granddad was relating, but I do recall a sudden confliction between vexation and pleasure. Vexation because Grandpa's yarn went unfinished and pleasure at the appearance of Mr. Mallik, one of my favorite people, who owned a small farm adjacent to Claremont; a gravel road separated it from Grandpa's orchard behind the house, which stood at the edge of town. I felt very kindly toward the old farmer because he let me indulge what Aunt Katherine called, "a dangerous impulse" to catch pigeons in his barn. I would climb the cleat ladder at the end of the haymow (now comes the "dangerous" part), swing hand over hand on the hayfork rail up in the very top of the haymow, climb up into the cupola where the pigeons congregated, and plop them into a gunnysack. If there was hay, I'd just drop into it. An empty mow necessitated a return on the rail, thrillingly scary for a six-year old — and as I think of it now, probably qualifying as dangerous.

Mr. Mallik was the picture of misery. Dirt and grease smeared bib overalls with patches on the knees and coming-apart, lace-up leather knee boots copiously smeared with cow dung framed the exhausted, beaten man. That evening he walked toward us head hung. He twisted a toe on the cement walk leading to the pump leaving an indelible, dark spot for many years: the dregs of a man squeezed by the relentless hand of the Depression. In halting, hardly audible phrases, Mr. Mallik made a plea to my grandfather to borrow a tractor for spring plowing, because, his tractor had fallen to such a state that it "thumbed its nose at repair. But," he added, "I've got seed," then, despair seemed to choke him as he whispered, "if I can find a drill." (A planter.)

Grandpa, not one to mince words, replied that never in a thousand years would he allow anything of his in the hands of a man that let his machinery sit out in the rain and consequently rust, ignored the needed paint on his barn, or tolerated such a filthy barnyard. On all counts, Mr. Mallik was guilty. He had a perfectly sound corncrib in which a tractor might be sheltered; at slow times, when he might have painted his outbuildings, he most likely could be found uptown, playing whist in the back of Jack Rand's hardware store; and as for sprucing up the barnyard, that couldn't be accomplished from the comfortable swing of a shade-splashed hammock, in which he was known to spend lazy summer afternoons.

However, I went to sleep that night wondering why Grandpa, who usually went out of his way to help folks, had been so quick to deny help to our neighbor. After all, Grandpa owned two tractors. Long before sunup, I awakened to creaking stairs. Quiet as a ghost, I slid from bed and watched Grandpa go out to the garage and back his Ford out to the road. About noon, he returned for lunch and I overheard him say to Grandma, ". . . that darn slacker doesn't have enough seed . . . be another fifty dollar trip to the elevator . . ."

I'll conclude this story by summarizing. Grandpa did Mr. Mallik's spring plowing, bought more seed, used his drill for planting, combined the wheat, and probably saved Mr. Mallik's farm from foreclosure that year.

In February 1950, Grandpa died and his funeral held on one of the iciest, windiest, cold and slippery days that I can remember (other than my mother's funeral). Mr. Mallik caused quite a stir in an "old folks home" in Owatonna when he went AWOL that day.

In his nineties, he slipped and hobbled the thirteen frigid miles to attend Grandpa's funeral. He was corralled at the church and taken back to the nursing home, but not before demonstrating a deed of thanks that shamed mere words.

grandfather—Grandpa had a big heart. When I was old enough to actually take note of adult interactions, I realized that some visitors came to the imposing house on Front Street whenever they or their cause needed financial help; Grandpa's generosity was well known. He was solid financially, selling casualty insurance in the mornings and working the farms until dark. I had heard adults surreptitiously remark on his honesty, such as, "He really is honest," or "Old Fred didn't cheat him, I couldn't believe it." Yet, I could never understand the niggling undercurrent of accusation, until much, much later.

Many of my family unwittingly conferred heroic virtues of generosity, industry, and honesty on my grandfather through a series of family stories; a couple follow.

Granddad and his younger brother, Ruben, traveled the Dakotas selling a line of blankets, scarves, and flannel knit goods (for North Star Woolen Mills, based in Minneapolis). One day, entering a South Dakota town, the brothers decided that one would canvass the north side of the main street, the other, the south side. In early afternoon, they met back at their hotel and Grandpa's success reduced his brother to tears because he had made no sales.

"Come on," said Grandpa, "we'll go back on your side together."

They called on the same retailers that had refused to buy from Ruben in the morning, and Grandpa not only convinced a couple of them to buy, but one sale was the largest either had ever made. To me, this yarn sounds a little like a Russian fairy tale; to the family, however, it was gospel.

However, I'm pretty sure this next Grandpa-is-a-great-guy story is true. Grandma and I would occasionally accompany Grandpa on his insurance calls. In one instance, after entering a large, neat farmyard, a teenage girl came running from the house, and as Grandpa exited the car, hugged him enthusiastically. She was followed by a sun-weathered man in faded bib overalls who extended a warm, two-handed handshake.

Grandma and I remained in the car. "That's him . . . him!" she whispered, "he's Grandpa's best customer now."

"The whip?" I whispered back.

"Yes."

I didn't need more explanation. I knew the story.

Grandpa had pulled into that same farmyard several years before, hoping to sell insurance to the owner, one of the county's most successful farmers. He found the man whipping his daughter (the hugging girl) on their back porch. (In my Claremont years, this was neither an unheard of parental act nor a particularly unusual disciplinary tool.) Never one to think a situation to death, Grandpa bolted from his car, commandeered the whip, and turned it on its previous user, "teaching the man a good lesson . . . trimming him nicely." Then, according to the story, he admonished the man to "Never put that whip near the girl again . . . or I'll be back." But he did go back, repeatedly. Whether from fear or repentance, the chastised man became a trove of insurance referrals and, per Grandma, his best customer.

I'm not totally enthralled by this tale. Unlike those recounting the incident, I do not see a 100 percent hero, rather half hero and half bully.

From my child's-eye view, I saw Grandpa in a slightly different light.

Not many argued with my grandfather; I did. Though he was intimidating—"If you were my boy, I'd cure you of . . . (fill in whatever annoyed him) in a hurry"—I knew he was all bluster. He never laid a finger on my father and loved children much too much to ever cause them pain. Though patently a stern and busy man, he found time for fun and pranks, like stuffing paper in the toes of my shoes as I slept. Abetting my love for wild creatures, he provided me with a steady procession of turtles gleaned from highways, owls plucked from the fields (too shocked to fly after farm machinery passed over them), and many other scurrying, slithering, flapping critters. In contrast, more than once my father said, "I saw a turtle on the road today . . . darn near stopped to pick it up for you," which was as close as he ever got to doing so.

When a second cousin of Grandma's died, leaving her small daughter in a farm household of boys and men, Grandpa (so I was told) insisted on including the young girl, Janet (see **murder**), in his household. She was like an older sister to me.

In faddish, current parlance, Grandfather might have been accurately described as a macho guy. But macho or not, as long as he possessed the strength to stand, he never failed his Monday ritual. Like many houses built at the turn of the nineteenth century, Grandpa's house possessed a stairway leading from the outside yard, into the basement. Its wide, limestone steps, covered by two large, slanted wooden doors opening from the middle, were seldom used except on Monday mornings: washday. It mattered not that planting, harvesting, or other urgent chores awaited him, on Monday morning, Grandpa would carry the washing up from the basement, for his beloved, and patiently hold the basket of laundry for Grandma to hang.

I witnessed a beautiful, loving exchange between Grandpa and Grandma during spring vacation in my senior year in high school. A classmate friend, Don Bushnell, owned a 1931 Plymouth Coupe and we drove it to Claremont, spending the week with my grandparents. Not long before that time, a massive heart attack kept Grandpa from the upper bedrooms, and he spent his nights in the office/parlor on a skimpy little bed that looked too narrow to accommodate a beanpole. He still walked around the house, but even a few minutes exhausted him.

One afternoon, Grandma listened as Don and I sat in the living room discussing whether or not to attend a movie in Owatonna. Grandpa appeared and said, "Here's five dollars, Frederick, why don't you take Mother, and you all go."

Immediately, Grandma said, "Oh, I don't think so . . . let the boys enjoy themselves alone."

"Come on . . . you'll like the movie," I said.

"No, no. I'll stay right here."

"If you're worried about me, I'll say goodbye now." Grandpa smiled. He clasped Grandma, who was standing, and planted a kiss on her forehead.

She pushed him away, to a conversational distance, and fixed her gaze on him. "I am not good at long-range. If you go, I want to be right here to say my goodbyes!"

Grandpa reclaimed her. Patting her, he said, "If you're going to be stubborn about it, Margaret, I won't 'go."

Good to his word, he waited another two and a half years to "go."

I did not learn of perhaps the finest example of my grandfather's generosity until long after his death, even several years after my father died. Unbelievably, my mother—through fifty-one years of marriage to his son and a several year residence in grandfather's hometown, a churning hotbed of gossip—had no knowledge of this incident until I pursued the chance remark of a Claremont "old-timer." Although I was in my fifties before I finally pieced together the episode, I clearly remember taunts of "your Grandpa's a jail-bird" from six-year-old playmates. The jibes, which at the time I assumed to be just ordinary playground teasing, were, half a century later, revealed as truth.

One of Grandpa's older brothers worked in a small town bank, and fresh from high school, Grandpa joined him there. Evidently, big brother and Grandpa "borrowed" bank funds to invest in stocks, their plan being to take the profit and then return the "loan." Not readers of Bobby Burns, they failed to reckon that even the "best laid schemes . . . Gang aft agley." Unfortunately, their scheme went about as "agley" as a scheme can "Gang," when, just before the bank examiner came, their stock took a tumble. Unimpressed by their entrepreneurial creativity, the law demanded its pound of flesh. I'm pretty sure (but, of course, it's pure supposition on my part) that eighteen-year-old Grandpa wasn't author of the scheme. Nonetheless, because his older brother had a wife and children, Grandpa took the sole blame and spent a couple of years behind the imposing walls of, Minnesota's Stillwater prison.

Three or four years before his death, Grandpa experienced chest pain and visited the Mayo Clinic. X-rays indicated a large, shadowed area. The diagnosis was fluid on the lungs. Adjudged a temporary condition, he continued ordinary daily activities. This included cleanup, after a minor farm mishap, that required shoveling up nearly fifty bushels of spilled wheat with a bushel scoop shovel. Probably too much for even a healthy man in his mid-seventies, it crippled Grandpa so severely that he never recovered. He spent his final two years wasting away in bed.

That x-rayed shadow, it turned out, wasn't fluid on the lungs, it was an enlarged heart. Yet, no one who knew him needed an x-ray to tell you that.

grandmother—I have been blessed with two guardian angles; Grandmother was one. Until the age of majority, she and her sister were my support system. I owe any shred of self to those two beautiful people who, in stark and constant contrast to my parents, loved me unconditionally. Their patience with an egregiously over-energetic child, who would have tried the toleration of a Miltown (meprobamate) medicated Saint, never, ever, flagged.

Grandma kept marks on her kitchen door, charting progress in the height department, read to me for hours at a time, patiently answered endless small-boy-type questions, packed scores of tasty lunches for all-day "creek-explorations," not only suffered with, but helped provide a home for an infinite menagerie that hopped, squirmed, or flew. She provided hundreds of glass-jar homes for tiny amphibians, fireflies, cocoons, etc. In my day, most jars came with metal caps and air-holes were punched into them with a hammer and nail; if I had a dollar for every time I cut my hands on the razor sharp, inside edges of the breathing holes, I could have retired before I shaved.

Like Joshua in the Bible, my grandmother crumbled Claremont's provincial walls, but with printed words. She must have read a thousand hours of Kipling, Scott, Porter, Burns, and others before my fifth birthday. She frequently read from *Commack's Choice Readings*; I shall never forget "Darius Green and his Flying Machine" or a story about an Irishman named Paddy, who went to a neighbor to ask for the loan of a griddle. On the way, he thought of a zillion reasons for which he might be refused. When finally reaching the neighbor, Paddy blurted something to the effect that he wouldn't borrow the griddle if the nonplussed neighbor begged him to. That was instructive of her teaching: don't borrow trouble.

Grandma was very much ahead of her time. She had, at the least, equal say on domestic matters, was president of the Claremont School Board and her reading club, did the family income taxes, and insisted that she and Grandpa maintain permanent, year-around living quarters in the Dunbar Apartments in Owatonna so that my father and his sister could receive the educational advantages of Owatonna's high school. She was sort of the grande dame of Claremont, but not so "grand" that she didn't sleep on the floor every night, summer and winter, alongside of a small bed in the "office/parlor" where Grandpa, totally bedridden, was confined for the final two years of his life. Grandmother spoke her mind on any subject, but accepted frustrations with graceful silence; the following two examples were most instructive to me.

I often stayed with my grandparents, and while there, spent considerable time at Mr. Mallik's farm (across the road from Grandpa's orchard). The brushy, mostly pine windbreak harbored copious bird life, which captured my attention for hours at a stretch. After supper was a good time for bird watching there, and because I would probably have stayed all night, Grandma's signal for me to come home was a couple of short honks on the Ford's horn. On one occasion, I simply ignored the signal. A second call, some ten minutes later, elicited a like response. It was well after dusk when a third set of honks propelled me home.

Grandmother stood outside the back door. "I honked several times," she said evenly, "didn't you hear?"

"I didn't hear until the third time." Dad was prescient about "stupid."

"Well, in future," Grandma said conversationally, "try and hear after the first time." There was no further rebuke, life simply went on. But I recall that when we went inside and had a dish of ice cream I tried to act normally — whatever that is for a six-year-old — but on the inside, I was smacking myself around worse than Dad ever did.

Thereafter, I would have eaten spiders rather than disappoint my grandmother.

Another example of her forbearance came after the second of two visits, bracketing a month or so, from one of Grandpa's many brothers. A big-city-dweller, our visitor explained that, "due to the Depression" (as though he was its sole, helpless target), he was in need of a very temporary loan. I recall sitting on the sofa next to Grandmother and she squeezed my hand when he said something to the effect that he had a sure-fire deal cooking. "Just temporary," he assured them, " . . . be back in thirty days with the money."

Grandpa, always a soft-touch for a hard-luck story, wrote out a check and accompanied his brother outside to see him off. I was packed off to bed, but not before I heard Grandma's even voice declare, " . . . due to more than . . ."

Not long thereafter, my great uncle returned, this time accompanied by his wife, who sported a luxurious, new fur coat. Smiles filled the living room while the Minneapolis couple were seated and served the obligatory coffee and pastry. Then, following an appropriate period of small talk, apologies were made, repayment was not. However, big-city brother assured Grandpa he was not to blame, it was the "darned Depression" that scotched his sure-fire deal.

The incident was a topic of intense family discussion, Grandpa and Grandma excepted, for weeks afterward; of course, I soaked up every word.

"Margaret (Grandma) just hates it when Fred (Granddad) does things like that."

I distinctly remember my mother's contribution: "He doesn't seem to give a *tinker's dam* about money, she should have *put her foot down.*"

"Especially . . . she wanted a new coat this year."

" . . . It's just not fair."

"Fair" or not, Grandma never volunteered a word on the subject, until I pried. "Janet (see **murder**) says Uncle Ruben spent the money on a coat and she thinks that's 'awful.' " The irony, though not the memory of her answer, was lost on me when I asked, "Do you think that was 'awful,' Grandma?"

"If I think about it at all, I won't need a new coat to keep warm."

great-aunt— Aunt Katherine lives in my heart, alongside her sister, as guardian angel number two. She read to me tirelessly, played endless games of Flinch and checkers, and entered my small-boy world of interests, as an equal, with enthusiasm and seriousness. She never returned condescending adult fire, though suffering a ceaseless barrage of childish questions.

"Why don't we learn that together?" was a frequent response. We would then sit at the dining room table while she consulted a red-covered volume from the encyclopedia set. I have no recollection of the question, but I clearly remember a particular encyclopedic answer: nocturnal Lepidoptera—night-flying moths. We even consulted the bright red tomes of knowledge when settling on a name for a stickleback minnow.

My tolerant aunt helped construct countless living arrangements for minnows, tiny toads, tree frogs, and other unfortunates. We'd start out with a cake pan or large dish filled with soil to a degree appropriate for the impending tenant, add a smaller container for water, some small plants and rocks, and presto, Aunt Katherine's kitchen side table would be transformed into a Lilliputian zoo.

The stickleback in question was gleaned from the County drainage ditch, where it entered our minor fork of the Zumbro river, on a Wednesday. Therefore, it wasn't much of a research project to look up Wednesday, in the encyclopedia, and find it named after a chief Teutonic God, Woden.

At the time, I really liked Woden. Looking back, had I really liked him, I wouldn't have collected him, but I was too young to understand that love does not necessitate possession. These days, I have mixed views of zoos; who am I to deprive others of the wondrous experience of close-up contact with exotic wildlife, yet my moral compass points to the inhumanity of imprisoning innocent creatures.

Morally incarcerated or not, Woden lived longer than most of my other captive creatures; having an "in" with the gods, even in name only, probably helped.

Thursdays were wonderful and aromatic: baking day. Now, some seventy-five plus years later, I can still hallucinate a bit of the smell of her fresh bread and black raspberry pies. I treasure the memory of warm, coarse-grained, fresh-from-the-oven bread, spread with Claremont creamery butter, but Aunt Katherine's specialty was mocca cakes, not mocha, as there wasn't a speck of coffee or chocolate in them. They were elongated cubes of white cake, covered with white frosting, rolled in unsalted, crushed peanuts, and individually wrapped in wax paper. Imitators were legion, but her's were heaven, others, distinctly terrestrial. No matter where I was, my parent's home, university, or in my own home, until shortly before her death the mail carrier would periodically deliver a package with Aunt Katherine's distinctive writing. Those packages would invariably contain mouthwatering mocca cakes along with many delicious memories.

My aunt's talents were not limited to kitchen triumphs. And, though her formal education ended with high school, her penmanship was exemplary, yet paled before her intellectual writing skills; to me, her letters are cherished works of art. Her first letter to me was written when I was thirteen days old. I cannot bear to share the majority of its contents, just the final snippet:

" . . . Today you received your first letter from your foolish old Aunt who is happy to be one of the number to welcome you into this big world with so much good in it and so much bad, and who hopes that you will absorb so much of the good that you will be able to fight hard, the bad. Lovingly, Aunt Katherine."

My beloved Aunt: I am not certain that we would, now, exactly agree on just what is good or what is bad, but I am certain that I arrived at my definition of good and bad by most of the moral principles that you taught.

hindsight — My somewhat myopic perception of past events is like an inverse zoom lens that widens the field of view, but then fiddles with the focus, highlighting embarrassing realizations of how much better life might have played out if only . . . However, underdeveloped hindsight has saved me from overblown angst about past miscues — a likely consequence of less than standard vision. Sub-par vision that, in earlier years, I blamed on Mother's lack of vigilance.

It was a winter during our stay in St. Louis, Missouri, when a Paramyxovirus decided my nine-year-old body was a dandy place to set up shop. Though house-calls were routine for physicians in those days, ibuprofen, acetaminophen, or antibiotics were still a couple of wars away; conventional treatment for measles consisted of two weeks bed rest in a darkened room. The doctor emphasized that I was to remain in bed, the single exception: bathroom trips.

"And the shades must be drawn at all times, Mrs. Blanch."

". . . Don't know how I'll keep him down, Doctor. How will he read in the dark?"

"Oh, goodness. No! He's not to read a line. He could have complications."

"Oh, my!" Mom winced at the word complications, a most threatening medical term. It was in the same league as susceptible, which she claimed my last walk to the library had made me. She had fussed and scolded on my return from the three mile round trip in a cold, sleeting rain.

"You should know better," she stormed, "now, you'll probably be susceptible."

Perhaps she was prescient; measles followed hard on the heels of her prediction.

It was evident that Mom had relayed fully the doctor's prescription to Dad. That evening, he came into my room, mumbled "two weeks" and, without even a glance, removed my bookcase and its contents. Had he afforded me a more generous intellectual attribution (other than "darn fool pea brain"), he might have guessed that the fruits of my recent susceptible trip to the library, two jungle tales by Paul du Chaillu, lay beneath my pillow.

Paul du Chaillu, a two-fisted explorer/writer of the late nineteenth century, held most young "pea brain" readers in excited thrall. His tales of bravely confronting and dispatching savage gorilla's with but a .45 in each hand made heady reading, which, if possible, I was not about to delay. In hindsight, du Chaillu might be horrified (I hope) to contemplate the wanton murder of his biological cousins.

During the two weeks of darkened confinement, I consumed the exploits of the French adventurer, beneath the sheets, with the aid of my small flashlight.

In hindsight, Dad wasn't all wrong about the "pea brain" business nor was Mom responsible for my intransigence. In hindsight, I clearly see the author of my vision difficulties.

home remedy — The home remedy I remember, and have used to good effect, lies on the scale of make-do medicine somewhere between a two-by-four splint and chicken soup. A week or so following my sixth birthday, shortly after we moved from Grandmother's to the Weber house, I was enveloped by whooping cough. My mother, who had never experienced the disease, was two-thirds into a pregnancy and I was promptly hustled back to Grandma's.

Between bouts of vomiting, I was ecstatic. I don't imagine Grandma completely shared my enthusiasm, but she welcomed me with open arms, literally. During my extended stay, most nights played out about the same. Violent spasms of wee-hour coughing brought Grandma to my side with a cool, wet washcloth that she wound around my throat. The wet cloth, over-wrapped with a large cotton towel and securely safety-pinned, completed the "treatment." Usually, within minutes, sleep replaced the cough. Grandma said that her mother employed the same method to tame an unruly cough.

Whooping cough left me with a tricky throat for more than a dozen years. Disruptive "barking" led to scores of hours, standing in hallways outside of school classrooms, desperately trying to suppress the reflex that caused my expulsion. In my day, there was no such animal as a school nurse, nor was much sympathy wasted on my condition. Quite a few teachers regarded my problem as a lack of discipline; more than once, I was advised to "learn a little self-control." Could I have found the textbook on self-control, I would have gladly memorized it—forwards, backwards, and upside-down. In sanguinary moments, I imagined those "educators" in a very hot place, their mouths eternally propped open, while someone tickled their throat with feathers, the penalty for coughing, a thousand years in boiling oil.

In her preschool years, my daughter, Susan, suffered from nocturnal coughing. Her mother ridiculed my first attempts to apply Grandma's home remedy, but the ridicule soon stopped, along with Susan's cough.

hometown—Claremont, Minnesota. Fading eyesight and failing cognitive acuity have reduced my powers of observation. However, aside from a couple hundred more residents than in the thirties, a few additional houses and "Hogfest 2010," a civic festival featuring attractions such as a Citywide Garage Sale, a Free Street Dance, and Dress Up a Hog Contest, I don't notice much change.

The few years spent there were, nonetheless, formative. I have previously confessed that Claremont is my "spiritual hometown." Yet, no inducement that I can imagine would ever lure me back to its provincial confines. Every house was glass, every attitude and moral precept rigid as granite, every deed scrutinized, and every belief channeled through either the Presbyterian or Catholic official filter (depending on which end of town you were domiciled). I owe an incalculable debt to fate for early release from the Claremont thought-gulag. (see **agriculture**)

honey—One winter in the mid seventies, while living in the woods (south of Annandale, MN), I bought a book on beekeeping. And, though I pretend to be a writer and push the printed word, honesty compels me to warn about the inherent dangers of the printed page. That darn book on beekeeping led to more than three hundred hives, a honey house, a ton of extracting and bottling equipment, and about ten thousand stings. (see **beekeeping**)

horse—It's difficult for me to think of horses without recalling an experience with Uncle Finley's horses. I think I was pressing age six when, following a bright spring day after Sunday school, I was present when Nance and Bess (Uncle Finley's team) received their modest Sunday ration of ground oats, amounting to no more than a handful from a barrel at the front end of the barn. I liked to play in the barn, and a few days after observing my friend's treat, I thought to provide them not a snack, but a banquet. Confident that I lavished Nance and Bess with an unexpected feast, I piled each box in the corner of their mangers high with ground oats, emptying the barrel. Although it took the better part of the morning, the oats was consumed with apparent gusto.

That afternoon Uncle Finley hitched his team to the buggy and clattered away toward "uptown." (Any trip to Claremont's half-dozen or so business establishments was always "uptown.") I guess the horses, as well as I, were most fortunate that they didn't die from my largess. The scours did not strike them until the fully loaded buggy was half way home. Having many times ridden in the buggy when the horses broke wind, I can only imagine them breaking into scours—a polite, perhaps slightly archaic term for animal diarrhea. After Uncle Finley cleaned himself as best he could in the barn, he stormed into the house where I was listening to Aunt Katherine read a story. I then listened to a furious uncle—for about ten minutes. I was certain I'd receive a demonstration in the many uses of a horse whip, but, of course, Aunt Katherine was having none of that. I recall but one other time that I heard my gentle, kindly Uncle Finley raise his voice; that was when I collected the eggs from a wren's nest in the hollow steel fence post by the barn—but that's another story.

hunger—Though the 1930's Depression was deep and hard and long, I never experienced hunger; I saw it, but didn't recognize it.

Alongside the grain elevator and railroad tracks, the Claremont of my day boasted a long abandoned stockyard complex constructed of aging gray timbers. A small-boy's paradise, no playground could have been better suited for keep-away-tag than the complicated series of contiguous animal pens connected by wide, still functioning gates. We played a game in the stockyard that required an "it" person to tag another, the tagged person then becoming "it." However, if any player touched the ground, they immediately became "it." The first "it" would let the players get a head start, and then everyone madly scrambled along the fences toward the nearest gate. When the "it" approached, we'd climb on the gate, and with a mighty shove, ride across to the opposite side of a pen. Two of our companions, brothers from one of Claremont's poorest families, were particularly adept at the game but occasionally became "it" because the younger of the two would sag to the ground and begin crying. Through his sobs, he would complain that he was hungry. This brought derision from the rest of us; both their stomachs were always round and distended, as though they had just finished a feast. Sometimes the brothers slunk away, to a chorus of "crybaby."

Many years passed before I realized that my playmates had been starving. I could have easily taken them to Grandma's or Aunt Katherine's for a sandwich, but didn't know enough to do so.

Another regret for my collection.

I

imitation — Strangely, creative efforts sometimes take on a life of their own. In the late nineteen-nineties, I wrote a piece for a harp, cello, percussion, trio. The work, "Minnesota Tango," was completely inappropriate for the Trio, but I couldn't seem to help myself; at that moment, I just had to write what was in my head, a piece for chorus and mime. (see Appendices, page 135.) What else might a Minnesota tango be, but shoveling snow? The Trio struggled through a single performance (I'm sure to humor me), demonstrating its uselessness as instrumental music.

I then submitted it to a well-known Minnesota humorist, thinking it might be a good fit for his radio show. Receiving no response after a couple of months, I called; the female voice (with whom I dealt on the telephone) said it would be returned "shortly." Another couple of months elapsed and I called again, this time with assurances that they "would find it." After a significant wait, I called a third time and the errant manuscript showed up in the mail a few days later, but I noted that my SASE (which writers send along with their submissions) wasn't used. Months later, I received a note from one of the Trio members for whom the piece was originally written, and who, coincidentally, had a connection to the well-known Minnesota humorist's radio show. Among other things the note said, "While paging through the . . . catalog, I saw this! Looks like [name of the well-known Minnesota humorist] 'stole' your Minnesota Tango idea!" Along with the note was a copy of an article and photo of the humorist, and the lyrics to "The Snow Shuffle."

Was I angry? Yes. Could it simply have been a coincidence? I don't know. Once before, I'd been victimized by "miraculous editorial coincidence." Did I care whether it was our iconic humorist or an associate who actually seemed to have this coincidental epiphany? No; visions of toiling litigation swam before my eyes. However, angry or not, I followed one of Mom's well-used dictums, "don't cut off your nose to spite your face," and rationalized away some of the "injustice" with another of Mother's favorite maxims: "imitation is the sincerest form of flattery."

imprecation — Cursing was taboo in my family. I heard my father swear but once. A model T flivver careened crazily toward us as we drove along a highway. Dad pulled to the side of the road and stopped, but, as though there were a bull's-eye painted on our side, the out-of-control vehicle smashed into us and bounced to the far side of the road. After much pounding and pushing, Dad managed to force open the crumpled door. He bounded from the car bellowing curses, referring to the high probability that the driver's unwed mother was of canine extraction; the arrival of onlookers silenced him. That was it, I never heard him utter another imprecation. Mother frequently used the expression tinker's dam; I guess she escaped swearing on a technicality. Grandma, Aunt Katherine, or Uncle Finley would have jumped from a high bridge rather than even think of cursing. Grandpa was a little less restrained; any tense situation revealed his wide-ranging grasp of colorful vocabulary.
Perhaps five, my first sally into the world of forbidden words was promptly rewarded by my Aunt Peggy. Using my ear as a handle, she dragged me to the sink and washed my mouth out with soap; it must have been an inferior brand, for it lacked efficaciousness.

improvise — The word "improv," if it is a legitimate word somewhere, isn't listed in any of my dictionaries. I am going to use it in the context of "improv-theater." For a few mid-life years, I had quite a lot of fun acting in (usually) dinner settings where our cast (actually, in two different loose casts) would put on a murder mystery, as the evening's entertainment for various organizations. It was fun because no rehearsals were required; just show up at the appointed place and time. The cast's impresario was paid; actor's pay was not munificent, usually a gourmet dinner, but the challenge of putting together a coherent plot, as we went along, kept most of us interested and coming back for more.

My most memorable moment was doing a show for a Jewish group, however, I did not know it was Jewish or what the group did or stood for, if anything in particular. To me, they were all strangers, just another audience. The gathering was at a fancy Minneapolis restaurant (at Riverplace) and after polishing off a really good filet mignon, I jumped from my seat, picked out a fellow sitting at an adjacent table, and screamed that he could hide no longer, accusing him of the posited murder. The shocked diners fell silent as I laid my hand on his shoulder and raved, at the top of my lungs, that, not withstanding his public persona of kindness and charity, I knew all about his dirty, underhanded double-life of debauchery and crime. I berated the man for at least five minutes, accusing him of just about everything from j-walking to pedophilia, all the while wondering why my audience wasn't laughing. Quite the contrary, not a fork journeyed to a mouth; not a glass clinked; most sat in stony silence, disbelief and shock freezing previously animated faces. I added that, as further proof of his culpability, the guilt on his face was as good as blood on his hands, "hell's fires" were in his future. This elicited gasps from the assemblage, and though convinced I had scored a thespian home-run, nonetheless took it as my cue to sit down and shut up. Such a babble ensued that the improv presentation was unable to continue; I was, for real, a "showstopper." With the unerring "luck" of the unprepared ignorant, I had singled out the group's Rabbi. One might think that the little incident with the Rabbi would have nudged me into considerations of less hit-or-miss pursuits. Not so.

I was literally "kicked out" of my acting career; it required a rather nasty incident to precipitate my retirement from trodding the boards. My "improv" swansong occurred very near my home, in Orono. Mid-summer, the impresario called and wondered if I would play a dead body. "It'll pay you twenty dollars," she said.

"What's the catch?"

"You'll have to lie on the ground by the railroad tracks in Spring Park . . . for about fifteen minutes." She explained that Pillsbury had engaged a dinner train for a group of its employees to have a breakfast on the train, which would go west for about eighty miles and, on the return, take in one of the standard murder mysteries that her group performed. "But you can't go, you've got to lay by the tracks as we pull away . . . so they can see your body."

She sounded like I was dead already. "When's it going to be?"

"September 26th."

"Can get kinda chilly by then."

"I'll make it twenty-five bucks."

How could I resist a twenty-five percent pay raise in five minutes?

"You've got to be there at 7:45 a.m. Train leaves at 8:00 sharp." She repeated, "Be lying on the ground alongside the second car at 7:45, not a second later!"

On the day of my "death," we experienced a premature frost. I arrived where the train was scheduled to leave (the station building had long before disappeared), and as far as I could see, the ground sparkled with silver frost. As instructed, I lay down by the second railcar and, method actor that I am, imagined how I would act were I really dead. In a few minutes, I was praying for death, for a release from the bone-crystallizing cold.

The first Pillsbury "jaunters" were a couple of middle-aged women who were obviously unfamiliar with the day's program. As they boarded the train, one of them said. "You'd think they'd pick up the filthy drunks before we got here." I cracked an eye open just enough to see her still pointing at me. I wished with all my heart that I had consumed that much alcohol; it might have made the cold more bearable. People straggled by for at least the next twenty minutes — so much for "8:00 sharp." At last, the train let out two short bursts of its horn that, were I dead, would have surely wakened me. Ears still ringing, I heard a voice say, ". . . don't believe it." Almost concurrent with the words, my ribs were stabbed with pain as a hard-toed boot drove into my side.

"Ow." I fairly screamed.

"Son-of-uh-bitch was fakin' . . . let's go!" My role forgotten, I sat, rubbing my side as a tall young man hustled a girl aboard and jumped up the steps of the railcar. Before I could rise, the train shuddered and jerked into forward motion. I do remember the scowling face of the impresario peering from the window of car number three as I raised my hand in a bon voyage wave; I truly don't remember how many fingers the salute included, but I'm sure she understood my resignation.

insurance — Upon graduation from university, I accepted employment from a relatively large company at a salary of $225 per month. I suppose the pay was about average, but I soon concluded that their employee relations' practices fell somewhere on a continuum between Byzantine galley oarsmen and Kamikaze service.

A bit about the company, as I perceived it, which has changed its name (smart move on their part) since my tenure there. I think Bob Cratchit might have suffered regrets, had he forsaken Ebenezer Scrooge's country club atmosphere for employment with (then) International Milling Company. Their stools might have been a trifle updated from Dickens's day, but, in my opinion, their employment practices might have paralleled those of Scrooge and Marley (e.g. keeping a tally of leaving one's desk; there was no air-conditioning, but windows were sealed and suit- jackets and ties decreed to remain on until temperatures hit around ninety — and even then the ties stayed put). I thought a fitting company motto would be "Bah! Humbug."

During my tenure, the Executive VP of the First National Bank, Mr. Malcolm McDonald joined the firm (which I'd guess he almost immediately deplored) as VP of Finance. In a burst of goodwill (and, I suppose, self-interest), First Nat. Bank sent over a dozen red roses to Mr. McDonald, the first morning of his new employment. Where a vase was dredged from is a mystery; the roses adorned his desk (everyone, from owner to pool secretaries, sat out in an open bullpen) for no more than an hour or so when, as scuttlebutt had it, word came down from on high that, at International Milling Company, such displays of frivolity were not tolerated. The roses disappeared; welcome to your new digs, Mr. McDonald!

At the time, I would have put my name on the dotted line for service in the Foreign Legion so it was an easy task for Gerry Franksen to recruit me into the life insurance business, as it played out, for a five year enlistment. Concluding my first year, I was awarded a trip to New York, and in a fancy ceremony, presented with a bronze and walnut plaque for selling more "lives" (policies) than any of the Company's thousand plus sales people. Plaques for achievement are a dime-a-dozen and I doubt that this one will get me a free pass at the pearly gates.

J

jack-of-all-trades, master of none — It's humbling to think of my life summed up in one, simple cliché. I dabbled at actor, beekeeper, composer, entrepreneur, printer, photographer, salesman, television producer, writer, and other enterprises, but was master of none.

job — Aside from a three week stint at Hilltop Nursery, Minneapolis, where I earned twenty-five cents an hour, paid in cash on Fridays, my first real job (with a check and payroll stub) was at a Firestone store in the Lake Hennepin area in Minneapolis, during sophomore year in high school. Most duties consisted of carrying auto and truck tires, by standing inside them, up rickety wooden stairs, from the basement where they were stored. Some of the tires nearly matched my weight which probably contributed to the two hernia operations in later years.

As the Christmas season neared, their delivery driver and sometime retail floor-salesman quit. I begged to take his place on the retail floor — and did I have fun! The incredulous manager generously awarded me a five-dollar Christmas bonus for racking up some astronomic sales — "Really great for a fourteen year-old kid with acne." Great that is, until after the holiday sales season when a good share of those sales were returned. The manager even hinted that my munificent bonus should follow my "sales" and be returned. Oh, ignominy! I spent the rest of my days at Firestone carrying tires up from the basement.

Near Yellowstone

kindness—This small odyssey of two teenaged boys exemplifies "kindness." It is a story that might just as well have been listed under "luck" or "unbelievable coincidence" — each equally applicable. I will try to confine its description to its most memorable events.

The summer between high school and university, my friend, Larry, and I planned to work our way around the western states, with visits to Canada and Mexico if we could fit them in. We prepared for months. We each bought a flexible travel-bag that accommodated one pair of jeans, two underwear shorts and two pair of socks, an extra T-shirt, and, with much wadding and prodding, a flimsy windbreaker. I wouldn't characterize the bag as small, only mention that it was a chore to squeeze in a toothbrush. There was no need to overcrowd my bag with a razor, but Larry's dark beard required daily maintenance. Antedating the "hippie" movement by more than a decade, young men expecting rides from strangers were clean-shaven.

Each girded with five dollars, our Odyssey began as the day dawned, in the glare of a Homeric proportioned, neon flying horse. The bright red Pegasus hovered above the Sinclair service station commanding the hilltop alongside US Highway 212, pathway to our western adventure. No longer a stop for motorists and long swallowed in the hustle-bustle of a thriving shopping center area just west of Minneapolis, in early June of 1947, the high-flying equine presided over rolling green pastures and plowed fields that mingled with groves of oak and basswood.

Hitchhiking was still quite acceptable. However, because of an occasional crime scare and slowly waning wartime camaraderie, it was no longer a "sure thing." During the War, "riding the thumb" was often the quickest and most direct transportation for servicemen; it was considered an unconscionable breech of patriotism to pass by military personnel with extended thumbs. In 1947, enough goodwill and American cohesiveness still survived so that Larry and I rarely waited more than a few minutes between rides.

Crossing Minnesota was, as they say, a piece of cake. We traversed most of South Dakota with a friendly semi truck driver to whom we "loaned" much of our cash. Another truck driver carried us from Spearfish, South Dakota to Cody, Wyoming. However, by late afternoon of the second day our luck seemed to run out, stranding us at a country crossroads, a few miles from the east entrance to Yellowstone Park. For several hours, no vehicle came by. We thought that, perhaps, the road behind us had closed. Our pessimism grew as the temperature fell and our thin windbreakers failed to help maintain our body heat. Our spirits sank lower than the temperature as treetops to the west pierced the sun. The silence was profound, save our chattering teeth.

"We're gonna freeze our ass off if we just stand here all night."

". . . Right as hell about that . . . should see what that sign says."

Fifty yards or so, on the gravel road running to the north, was a small oblong sign. Peppered with bullet holes, it was unreadable, even up close, except for a possible mileage notation: "3."

"Looks like three miles to somewhere. Let's start walking," said Larry, ". . . no, there!"

"Wait, look!"

We had seen the light at the same moment. A half-mile or so away, a vehicle had turned onto the east/west road, heading in our direction. We ran back to the intersection, thrust out our thumbs, and but a few seconds later, a very old car rolled to a stop. The passenger door swung open revealing three large, unkempt looking fellows of about our age.

The driver, the largest of the trio, drawled, "Ya got money?"

Our goose is cooked, I thought, hope these guys don't have a gun. "Damn little . . . practically nothing," I said, "we're working our way around." That was true; we had spent nearly all our funds.

The backseat passenger asked, "You guys hungry?"

"Sorta," said Larry. We were ravenous. We had eaten in Cody and, two or three hours later between rides, had a bottle of Coca Cola®.

"Well, I could eat the ass offin uh heffier, but we're plum broke too," said the backseat passenger.

72

The driver said, "Git in . . . place sells groceries t' terists couple mile up the road." We got into the rear seat, the car backed a few feet, turned, and headed north. In the few minutes before a light beckoned from the "terists" store, Driver averred that there were "more lace hankies in uh pigs ass" than jobs in Johnson County. That was the sum total of intimate detail we learned about our hosts. But, friends in adversity, we pooled our money, bought a loaf of bread and a can of spam, and returned to the Plymouth.

1947 "Ensenada . . . a sleepy fishing village."

"Where you all from?" asked Backseat.

Larry and I answered in a single voice. He said, "Minneapolis." I said, "Minnesota."

Driver turned around and stared. He pulled an enormous hunting knife from his belt sheath and pointed it at me. It bobbed menacingly as he spoke, "Where you say ya . . ."

The backseat crowded three of us tightly; I could feel Larry stiffen. I think my heart stopped. Oh, God! Are we gonna die here, flashed into my head. I interrupted quickly, "Minneapolis . . . Minneapolis, Minnesota!"

The knife moved toward me. "Here . . . it were mostly yer money . . . you kin divvy up the spam." I heard my heart banging in my ears; blood began to circulate again as I accepted the knife. Driver was no killer, just honest and generous.

Front-seat Passenger spoke through a mouthful of spam sandwich. "Mah daddy usetuh tell 'bout them Minnesotas havin' football an' all . . . prairie dogs er some such . . . hey, you ever seed Ol' Faithful?"

"No."

"Well dammies!" said Front-seat Passenger to Driver, "Whyent we jes skip over there?"

"Too damn dark t' see much."

Backseat chimed in. "Gotta sleep summers . . . let's show these here boys."

"That's uh fact," said Driver, "Ahm with it."

We drove for a while and came to Yellowstone's east gate. In those days, I guess no one worried about grizzly thefts; the gate was open. I don't remember how long it took to reach the main lodge, less than an hour, I think. We expected lights, but the lodge hadn't opened for the season. We parked close by the large building and spent the night in the car. Our hosts possessed two thin blankets or we might have frozen.

In the morning we watched Old Faithful spit up a few times. Then we drove to West Thumb, appropriate, for after thanking our benefactors for their hospitality, we limbered up our own thumbs, and caught a ride with a very nice Mormon man and his daughter. We accompanied them all the way to Salt Lake City.

*   *   *

We stayed a few days in Los Gatos with my Aunt Peggy and Uncle Frank, then went on to Larry's Uncle Fred in Los Angeles. We were out of money, so we worked alongside migrant workers halving apricots and spreading the cut fruit on four-by-eight sheets of plywood, to dry in the sun. Uncle Fred took us to a racetrack. He and Larry made gentle fun of me for not betting the favorites to win, but conservative as ever, I bet the favorites to "show" and made a few dollars. Since then, I have adopted my insurance supervisor's strategy of only betting on "cinches and hunches," which limits my wagering activity to nil.

From Los Angeles we hitchhiked past San Diego, entered Mexico and went on down to Ensenada. I understand that, today, the Baja peninsula bustles with tourists and activity; then, it was dusty countryside and Ensenada no more than a sleepy fishing village. While there, we ate tamales purchased from a street vender's cart; drank the local water, which we were warned against, but must not have been lethal as I've managed to soldier on for nearly sixty-five years since.

Following another day's stay with my Aunt Peggy, we thumbed our way up the West coast and, just so we could say we saw Canada, crossed into Vancouver. Passports were not required in those innocent days. Returning south, once again we got a ride in Portland, squeezing into an ancient Plymouth with a family. The father drove, the mother, holding an infant, sat in the passenger's bucket seat, and two older children shared the back. Larry and our two duffels joined the kids in back, and I shared the bucket with the poor mother who was crowded nearly onto the high shift lever rising from the floor.

"I owe," said the driver, "I thumbed all over during the war, never took a bus . . . By God! I owe."

I remember thinking that his poor wife, and her backside, was paying a big share of that debt.

We rode with the family all night and the driver even bought us breakfast. And, though we might have continued further south with our benefactors, at a gas-stop in Canyonville, Oregon, we decided we had inconvenienced them enough. We departed the generous folks without ever learning their names.

We washed up in the service station's restroom, which I recall as tiny and extraordinarily dirty. Outside, we arranged a ride with a flatbed-semi driver who had stopped for gas. Larry took a seat, directly behind the cab, outside on the truck's empty bed. I got the cab, having to bend my legs and put my feet on the dashboard, as the passenger side floor was heaped with logging chains and topped by our gear.

The truck had barely gotten up to speed when it became apparent to me that the trucker was either crazy or suicidal or both. He careened the long vehicle around hairpin curves that would have challenged a sedately operated sports car. He swerved toward an approaching motorcycle, nearly forcing it over the sheer edge. Luckily for us, he was just crazy. He opted out of suicide, as he lost control around a sharp bend and chose to run through a telephone pole on the mountainside, rather than fly the thousand or so foot drop over the opposite roadside.

In an infinite flash, the mountainside, trees and brush, and the pole all seemed to crowd into the cab through the shattering window. The heavy chains shot forward, right through the steel flooring. I'm sure I would have followed, and been shredded, had not my feet, wedged to the dashboard, held me in place.

Larry had been flipped into the air and landed on the road, unconscious, but moaning. Fortune, who had momentarily turned her back on him, smiled; she sent a nurse in the first car to come by following the accident. The next vehicle was a pickup truck. Larry was laid on the truck's bed, I retrieved our bags, and we drove to the next town, with a hospital. The accommodating pickup driver, who had been traveling in the opposite direction, helped me lay Larry onto a sort of loading dock at the hospital.

A nurse appeared, examined the now conscious Larry, and explained that they could not accept indigent patients. Ironically, Larry's dad was in the insurance business, and my friend was the only person I knew that had some sort of health insurance, an almost unheard of commodity in those days. In spite of our assurances that they would be paid, and notwithstanding Larry's neck hardware identifying his religion as the hospital's, he was refused admittance.

Then, Lady Luck practically kissed him. Margaret Winters, a nurse, who had been making a delivery to the hospital, had been observing the non-admitting procedure, and furious at the hospital personnel, barked at the now small crowd to help her get Larry into her station wagon. We drove up to Roseburg and managed Larry into the elevator of the small, vine-covered, three-story building, where Larry stayed in a doctor's office overnight.

Margaret Winters worked in the lab across the hall.

No broken bones, but black and blue with bruises, the patient was released the following morning to the care of the nurse's friend, May Crow, a colleague in the lab. May had gasped a little upon first seeing me, then insisted I stay with her and her husband, Jim. She nearly fainted when she met Larry. "It can't be . . . can't be!" May sagged against her nurse friend for support.

In those days I was blonde and light, Larry very dark haired. May had lost her two sons in the War. Miraculously, not only was one son fair and the other dark, but their pictures showed an uncanny resemblance to both my traveling companion and me. We stayed with May and Jim for almost two weeks. May didn't want to let us go, but with copious tears all around, the Crows finally de-

Medical Art Building, Roseburg, Oregon. I recall this building as vine covered in 1947. Pre-World War II car suggests photo may have been taken years earlier.

posited us alongside the highway heading south, with instructions to call May's parents in Fresno.

Not only were May's parents ancient (I suppose about my present age), their house was a neat-as-a-pin relic of the Gold Rush. Their car — I could kick myself for not noting its manufacturer — had cut glass vases that hung from silver colored chains, just in front of the forward doors. We stayed overnight with them and were treated to a novel method of dividing labor. May's mother prepared a nice supper, and following, she and her husband played a game of cribbage to determine who would do the dishes. The loser said, "How about two out of three." Their game was still in progress as Larry and I settled into sleep.

I haven't seen Larry in a number of years, but I am reminded of him, and our small odyssey, every time my back twinges, a remnant of that ride into a mountainside.

L

lesson—Every experience may be interpreted as some sort of lesson. The following three incidents greatly influenced my economic life.

1.—My first bicycle was also one of my first and finest lessons in the world of finance and contract. This anecdote might belong under "strings attached," but because of its influence, belongs in a place of honor in my personal Pantheon of Economic Education Experiences.

Shortly after I turned ten, I recall dancing around the subject of a bicycle with Dad. The result was the promise, a genuine, "That's a promise" type promise of a bicycle for my twelfth birthday. The wait seemed unbearably long; nevertheless, I was elated. Even at that tender age, I realized that instant gratification moved out of our house when we (read Dad) moved in. When cornered by a request from a family member to go somewhere or pursue some activity, his invariable response was, "We'll do that someday." Variations on "someday" were "next year" or "I'll think about it." Someday never quite materialized. Next year's vague footprints were too difficult to track. And, this is just an opinion, very little thought seemed applied to bothersome requests, once one of the magic phrases dismissed the subject.

But this time there was a promise. A real I-got-your-hide-nailed-to-the-barn-wall-now promise. A certifiable, no wiggle room, verifiable date-of-delivery promise!

The big day finally came, and as always, Mom baked a nice birthday cake. Horrors, she could only rustle up eleven candles, and I agonized that latent lawyer Dad might notice and cop-out on a technicality. Blessedly, he didn't remove his nose from the evening paper long enough for a glance. From the dining room table, I kept an eye on him while unwrapping a pair of socks.

"Those are from both of us, of course," said Mom.

I could stand the suspense no longer. "Where's the bike, Dad?"

"What bike?"

"The bike you promised."

"You're the darndest kid I've ever seen. There isn't any bike."

"But you promised!" I shrieked.

"Don't you yell at me or I'll come in there and give you something to really yell about."

Dad's commitments might have been idle, but his threats were not. Still, I couldn't resist a sullen, but emphatic, "You promised!"

He slammed down the paper and stalked into the dining room. I stood and awaited the usual hard slap across the side of my head.

"I promised you that you could have a bicycle on your twelfth birthday, not that I'd get you one."

Zapped by the parental fine print again! I must have looked so miserable that even Dad's less than robust paternal conscience was piqued. "Tell you what," he said, "you put in half and I'll get the bike . . . no, I'll do better than that." Once the floodgates to his parental largess opened, there was no stopping the outpouring. "I'll get you the bike now and you can pay me for the half when you earn the money."

Overwhelmed by his unaccustomed generosity, I groaned a barely audible, "You're all heart."

"What's that . . . you being a smart mouth again?"

I saved wear and tear on whatever part of my anatomy stood closest to him as I mumbled, "No . . . no, Sir. . . . said it's a good start." He must have believed me because the next day, when he came home from work, his Chevy bore the finest twenty-four dollar Hiawatha bicycle carried by Gambles Hardware Stores.

The only bike I ever owned, I struggled with that incredibly difficult to pedal piece of junk for years. However, it did an admirable job of strengthening my legs, as well as strengthening my understanding of the bargaining process.

Lesson: examine a contract's fine print like an unknown mushroom; ambiguity may be poisonous.

2.—It was nearly 5:00 a.m. when my parents dropped me off at a roadside stand fronting endless, green stretches of raspberry fields. A man emerged from the tiny shed, introduced himself as the foreman, explained the intricacies of berry picking (consuming at least forty seconds), and outfitted me with the picker's single implement.

The tool of my new trade, a "lug," was a shallow, oblong wooden tray equipped with a wood handle at the balance point.

"Best t' carry it on yer arm 'stead uh yer hand . . . easier t' get the berries in tuh the boxes."

I was more accustomed to orders than explanations; it made me feel very "grown-up." Of course, I couldn't imagine that he opened the door to a singularly important life instruction.

During World War II anything resembling a warm body was a shoo-in for employment, which is, no doubt, why the proprietors of the large raspberry fields in Hopkins, MN permitted tender-aged youngsters to harvest their fragile crops. Anyone with eyes could see the squashed berries on the ground between the green rows. Anyone with common sense understood that "berry fights" generated the waste. Nonetheless, most adults weren't simple-minded enough to fill their fingers full of stinging barbs and court a desiccated demise by baking in dusty shadelessness for two dollars a day tops, achieved only if one forsook rest or horseplay. So, most pickers were feckless kids. "Nerdy," "straight-laced" kid that I was, my mission was labor to make money and labor I did. The money part, sort of.

Remuneration hinged on piecework in its most elemental form. One filled wafer thin, one-quart wooden boxes, just slightly over the brim, with delicate, blood-red, undamaged fruit—plus a small contribution of one's own blood, courtesy of the raspberry thorns. No one cared, with the possible exception of the picker, as blood was indistinguishable from crimson berry stain. When eight quarts of berries filled the lug, it was turned in to the foreman and the picker received a "twenty-five cent ticket" and a lug with eight empty boxes, beginning the harvest process anew.

Working from 5:00 a.m. to the 2:30 p.m. quitting time, pausing only briefly to squat in whatever narrow band of shade the sun allowed or to drink from the faucet outside the foreman's shack when bringing in a lug, I could accumulate eight, twenty-five cent tickets. That was par, which I did not always reach.

One warm, humid evening, following a "par" day, my parent's enthusiasm for my earning prowess resulted in rare permission to "bolt the reservation" and attend a neighborhood carnival held in Pershing Field a mile or so from home. Loaded with hotdogs and cotton candy, the crowd jostled and elbowed to popular entertainments like the merry-go-round, games of chance ("fat-chance" there'd be many winners), and the tilt-a-whirl. Only a few folks were queued for the Ferris wheel, to which I purchased a fifty-cent ticket.

A scruffy looking fellow took my ticket and I ascended a wooden step to a tiny platform at which the rocking seats paused to empty or acquire riders. I entered at either the end or the beginning of a full load. Consequently, the "ride" stopped to empty or fill every seat behind me, jerking around its course in spurts of a yard or so, never making an unbroken cycle. As I reached the bottom of the jolting circumvention, the carny opened the gate and said, "Let's go, kid."

"But I haven't had a ride yet."

"Ya been all the way around, ain'tcha?"

"Yeah, but . . ."

"Then git outta there and let these nice folks on."

A couple with a girl about my age were waiting to board and looked daggers at me. Adding insult to insult, as I stepped from the platform, the carny commented to the couple, loud enough for me to hear, "Damn kids got no respect these days."

I smoldered at the injustice for a day or so, and then, in the berry field, fingers smarting from the rasps of those darn berries and sweat pouring into my eyes, Eureka, epiphany struck.I had seared my fingers with tiny barbs and endured at least two hours of parched misery in exchange for five minutes of . . . fun? The idea nearly made me a miser. Fortunately, profligacy balanced that new found parsimony and left me with simple caution.

Lesson: labor pain is not exclusively feminine—equate expenditure to its labor equivalent before making a purchase.

3. — A friend, with whom I shared an epic journey through the Western States, Canada, and Mexico, by thumb (see **kindness**), shared my interest in birds and nature. We also ran muskrat traplines in the swamps bordering the south edge of Minneapolis. In the early 1940s, muskrat lodges dotted the marshes and shallow ponds nestled between sandy hills, in the present Fifty-sixth Street and Penn Avenue South area. I have only a fuzzy recollection of how we removed the poor beast's heads, turned them inside out over a stretching board, scraped away the innards, and rubbed salt on the

critically important whitish hide. Trapped out of season, muskrat hides appear greenish, in-season, white, which is the basis of this account.

At the end of our first trapping season, my parents drove Larry and me down to the fur district, somewhere around First Avenue North, just off Hennepin Avenue, in Minneapolis, with our harvest of fur. Dad pulled into a parking space directly in front of a fur dealer and Larry and I carried our season's bounty into the store. After looking over our hides, the fur buyer offered us a price for all the pelts save one. It was the very biggest, with the most beautiful fur.

"Can't buy that one," he said, "you got it out of season."

"No. No I didn't." I probably replied a little hotly because all the pelts were legal. We only trapped in season.

"It's green," the buyer said, "look there!"

I hadn't even known that out-of-season pelts were greenish. Vehemently, I said, "I can't help it, that pelt was trapped in season!" "I'm still not gonna buy it, kid . . . ya wanna argue, why don't you guys just beat it."

Disappointment was an understatement. We were devastated. Did my big mouth get us in trouble again?

Gathering the pelts in our paper shopping bags we shuffled out of the store. Then we noticed a man waving from inside the large plate glass window of a business across the street. I don't remember the name, but it was another fur company. As soon as we entered, the man came up to us and asked, "What's the matter, boys, Hy didn't offer you enough?"

I felt like I stretched the truth, but still, technically, the answer was, "No, sir."

"Well, let's take a look." He dumped the hides out of the bags, took a cursory glance and said, "Give ya two and uh half bucks apiece."

Lesson: a closed mouth can sometimes make the best deal.

love — A noun that would be better off as a verb. A lovely abstraction, it makes a better action than a mere thing, like a shirt, however, it is just as readily changed or, as in my case, "sent to the cleaners."

luck — I attribute the lion's share of whatever modest successes I've experienced to my silent partner. She found people to make up for my ignorance in projects I should never have undertaken. She steered emancipators to me, like Jerry Franksen, who helped extricate me from self-imposed serfdom, and D.J. Willis, who shared a lifetime of business lore. She introduced me to Opal Mathson Fisher's patient encouragement of my meager musical abilities, and arranged a meeting with Maureen Taube LaJoy, writing teacher par excellence. She guided my steps to a generous Yamaha piano salesman, Ralph Bauer. Ralph volunteered the use of Yamaha pianos, enabling me to develop and produce television programs of chamber music, a project superlatively facilitated by Barbara Nolan Clark and Marsha Patton—very fortunate introductions.

Though platonic, I have enjoyed a lifetime of passionate embraces by Lady Luck.

maternal grandparents — see **mother**.

Menière's syndrome — Lousy stuff! It's a goof-up of the inner ear and leads to surprise bouts of indescribable nausea, extreme dizziness, followed by the loss of one's last three Thanksgiving dinners. It's often labeled Menière's Disease, but is no more communicable than a large nose — though possibly passed on in the same way. I was plagued with it until an operation on my ear put an end to it, along with hearing in that ear. I'd gladly give an ear, or a leg and several fingers to be rid of the scourge.

mentor — "Better lucky than good." I cannot place the specific date in February of 1958 that proved to be hugely lucky for me, the day I met D. J. Willis, who would provide a priceless, practical business education, and become landlord, adviser, and mentor.

Restless in retirement, after many successful years operating D.J. Wills Credit Jewelers, Mr. Willis reentered the economic fray when he purchased a jewelry business in north Minneapolis, where I rented a tiny second floor room, the first home of Screencraft, (see **business**). Again, good luck prevailed immediately, keeping me busy making sales calls, estimating job costs, and delivering completed orders during daylight hours, and working in the shop with Willy Fry, my partner, until 2:00 or 3:00 in the wee morning hours. Then, on to home where I spent a half-hour or so cleaning paint from my hands, to look presentable at my 8:00 a.m. sales calls. (Right here, I'll credit Willy, and his technical experience, for getting me established in the silk screen printing business.) Describing that time as hectic is an understatement, therefore, it was a nettlesome interruption when our chatty old landlord cornered me to deliver one of his "war" stories.

At first, I listened simply to be polite. However, I soon concluded that my loquacious landlord offered a cornucopia of business lore that was open for the taking — in this case, listening. As our acquaintance and rapport grew, I would occasionally share a business problem.

In September, I confided my frustration at the inability to secure a bank loan for a machinery purchase. D. J. asked a few questions and abruptly stood, saying, "Let's go. " He grabbed my hand, literally, led me to his car, and drove us to the imposing Northwestern National Bank in downtown Minneapolis. There, with no apparent appointment or even a knock on the door, we entered the spacious office of the (or a) startled executive vice-president, Pat Clausen.

Barely across the threshold, Mr. Willis said, "Pat, I wancha t' meet uh kid that-ul be uh money mak'in' customer for ya."

A distinguished, graying-at-the-temples man in an expensive looking suit rose from his desk and thrust out a hand. He nodded, but remained silent as I managed a whispered, "Nice to meet you, sir."

Mr. Willis did not whisper. "I never seen a goyum verk like dis kid . . . do yerself a favor an' give 'im what he wants." He turned to me and said, as much for Mr. Clausen's ear as mine, "An' Freddy, you don't give um no chattel mortgage either . . ."

I didn't. With surprisingly little "paperwork," the loan went through without a hitch. However, a few weeks later, a young man called for an appointment, explaining that the bank wanted to "go over my books." I possessed no books, save a filthy, coverless copy of *Gulliver's Travels* left in the bathroom before our tenancy. However, the bank's auditor, J. Robert Kelly, pronounced Screencraft's records, kept on a hundred or so sheets of letterhead paper, satisfactory. He then did his best to explain P & L and Ledger statements, and that further loans would be conditioned on keeping financial records in those accepted accounting formats. As I am impervious to mathematical machinations, I hired an accountant—which also saved my backside the following income tax season.

A further benefit of D.J.'s introduction to the bank was the friendship I developed with J. Robert Kelly. A year or so following his examination of our "books," Bob left the bank. However, our relationship flourished. We have enjoyed the past fifty plus years as the best of friends, and still meet for lunch every couple of weeks. I fondly remember Mr. Willis and his countless sayings, like, "There are two people you always gotta tell the truth, your wife and your lawyer." Good student that I am, I have always followed that injunction—at least about fifty percent of it.

No recitation of my journey could be complete without acknowledging my gratitude and profound respect of Mr. D. J. Willis, landlord, adviser, and mentor.

metaphor—Many poems contain metaphor and some poems are metaphors.

Metaphor

'Twould strain my wit past incredulity
To think a scene more beautiful:
A nest of Robins in an apple tree.

Read the complete poem in appendices, page 142.

mother—Mother was born in 1899, in a sod house, somewhere in Kansas—she had a heck of a time convincing the Social Security Administration that she was a real person. Had she not proved the existence of my sister and me, said government agency might have argued that she was simply a figment of her own imagination. Luckily, for family continuity, she proved to be more corporal than imaginary.

Possibly more imaginary than corporal, however, was her assertion that her ancestors "came over on the Mayflower." The notion had been drilled into her by her imperious mother, who claimed that the distinction had been handed down "by mouth" from generation to generation. Dad said that if everybody who claimed Mayflower passage was actually on board, "The darn boat would have sunk at the dock." Mother steadfastly clung to the belief, having jumped from the frying pan of her mother's bullying into the fire of my father's caustic sarcasm, she was skilled at self-deception. Perhaps that is why she lived by clichés and aphorisms—one could not be criticized for the accepted conclusions of "Society."

Her father, a carpenter by trade (whom Dad derided as a "failed wood-butcher") would have preferred to raise flowers, which he loved, but was harangued or shamed into other pursuits, at which he failed. Her mother kept the family afloat by selling needlepoint art pieces to Marshall Fields in Chicago. I saw very little of my maternal grandmother, but I remember that she affected a solicitous but condescending sweetness that frightened me, and I was always relieved to leave.

Mother put herself through Oberlin College and then put as much distance as she could between her mother and herself. She found employment with General Electric, in Schenectady, New York, and worked her way to some sort of minor executive position—an extraordinary feat for a woman at that time.

I never could figure out why she married, and particularly, why she married Dad. It's my opinion (of suspect value) that she rationalized bullying as affection. The consequence of picking a lifemate so similar to her dictatorial mother was to adopt a flighty, scatterbrained ignorance as a defense mechanism against Dad's relentless verbal assaults, such as belittling her considerable artistic efforts, association with woman's organizations, that he labeled "hen clubs," and generally disparaging any of her non-domestic projects as "stupid."

Her secondary defense against criticism was to drown it before it was voiced. She talked incessantly about anything; she confided both personal and mundane family matters to complete strangers, even to me. If she told me once, she said a hundred times that she should "never have had children." She repeatedly referred to my "accidental" birth ("though you didn't come along until a year after we were married") and the attendant sacrifice she had endured. Rather than love me as a son, I believe mother took pride in my accomplishments, limited as they were, as a reflection of herself. During one of our mother/son discussions, shortly following my university years, I made her cry when I persisted in asking if she loved me. I give her credit for honesty, she simply could not say what she did not believe.

She seemed much closer to my six-years-younger sister, and patiently sat next to her on the piano bench for several years of lessons and, among other enterprises, actively entered in activities such as scouting. Fortunately for my sister's relationship with Mother, the complications of extended family were mostly absent.

Mom suffered from (was pushed into) a completely unjustified inferiority complex. Blessed with artistic talent, she could paint, sew, or decorate food with extreme skill. She was a reader with a consequently large vocabulary (though not approaching Dad's—which he was quick to point out), and took a lively interest in world events.

For most of my growing-up years, Mom was on a "diet." Until my father died, mother was what some might characterize as "pleasingly plump." Actually, she was quite a bit overweight. Dad caller her fat, but upon his death she slimmed down to normal. I suspect her weight situation was just another manifestation of her passive aggression. Outliving Dad by nearly twenty years, she demonstrated confident independence, tending beautiful gardens, and finally learning to keep a checkbook, though not accurately. She never regained the confidence to tackle driving in the city.

Another albatross in my lavaliere of regrets is my failure to reach a more intimate accord with Mother. Nature bestowed many common attributes upon us, among which, a mutually meager inclination for sharing exchanges.

Mozart Festival — In 1997, the Council Oak Trio of Tulsa, Oklahoma commissioned me to write a musical work that would serve as their signature piece, to be premiered at the fourteenth International Mozart Festival in Bartlesville, Oklahoma, June 12-20, 1998. If the location seems remote for an international conclave, the reason is simple: oil money.

The Trio's name intrigued me, and upon investigation, I discovered that the original Council Oak tree still stood in Tulsa, Oklahoma, surrounded by a small iron fence. It was a meeting place (tulwahaafe) for the Creek Indians following their 1834 expulsion from Alabama. The music was intended to represent various eras of activity surrounding the iconic tree. "Council Oak: Tulwahaafe," a piece in four movements for recorder, flute, clarinet, bassoon, and narrator, played to a packed venue and enthusiastic reception. I was invited to do the narration and received a grant from the Minnesota State Arts Board to attend. Following the presentation, a grizzled, but diamond-ring-bedecked, oil-man came out of the audience and asked me if I had ever worked on an oil rig.

"No," I answered.

"Well, ya mustuh . . . some other life."

He then stunned me with a nearly perfect quote of the narration introducing the third movement: "Gusher."

"How else wouldja knowed that 'one ache worseun the backache ya get from roughneckin' a drill crew, is the heartache' . . . er that 'good luck always seems t' be just a section away er another hundred feet down?'"

I didn't tell him that composers and writers are just full of baloney and lucky guesses.

murder—Janet was already a fixture at Grandma's when we moved back to Claremont and became part of the household. She was ten years my senior and became an instant "big-sister." She frequently, and accurately, called me a brat, but listened to my stories, occasionally read to me, and introduced me to interesting things—like taking a salt cellar out to the swing in the arbor, by the orchard, and stuffing down enough green apples with salt to get a stomach ache for a week. And slathering butter, pepper and salt on one's baked potato skins—a delicacy I relish to this day.

Over the years, we went our separate ways; she married (a fellow not my type) and I married and married. When her husband died, we became close again, mutually enjoying books and music. During her working years, Janet taught lower grades and, after her retirement, assisted with various projects to help disadvantaged youngsters.

A family party was planned for her seventieth birthday, her children gathered, and preparations were completed for the affair. A day or two before the event, she was assaulted in her home, we surmise (according to her stricken memory) by some of her disadvantaged youngsters, kicked and beaten into unconsciousness, living but a day or so, and unable to accurately identify her attackers. Police characterized her murder as a "robbery gone bad" and wrote it off as unsolved.

I still relish baked potatoes, and though my memory is a long way from perfect, each time I spread butter on baked potato skins, I think of my "big-sister."

N

narrate—The speed at which a story is told.

never—A word I should never have thought, or articulated. As a six year old, watching Uncle Finley carefully removing Christmas gift-wrapping from a box of chocolate covered cherries, I distinctly recall promising myself to "never, never get that old." The kindly old man's trembling, blue-veined hands, smeared with dark brown "horrid-age-spots" were repulsive talons ¬– I certainly didn't want to ever look like that. But, of course, that could never happen to me, never!

One of the very few things eight decades has taught is to never say never. Now, I'm older than Uncle Finley was when I vowed to never reach his age. Never satisfied, I probably would complain about the alternative.

obedience — If Moses could wander in the wilderness for forty years and still see Canaan, I suppose it's not unreasonable to expect pre-adult children, who wander in the wilderness of "teendom" for but half a dozen years, to ultimately see redemption. I confess that I am one of the " . . . ye of little faith;" I experienced moments when I feared daughter Susan might linger in the transitional teen-time desert forever, but, butterfly-like, she emerged from the cocoon of solipsistic teenage as a generous, loving, and caring person.

Susan and I went shopping together for her thirteenth-birthday present at Crossroads Shopping Center in St. Cloud. She knew exactly what she wanted, a stereo set, right down to the model number. Stereo was not exactly a cutting-edge electronic wrinkle in 1975, but most teens of moderate financial circumstances just "had to have a stereo" if their life was to have a shred of meaning!

My daughter's new system was little more than a radio with stereo amplification, outfitted with a vinyl-disk record player and two separate speakers. It came packaged in several cartons, and immediately after bundling them into the car Susan said, "We'll get it going soon's we get home?"

"I can't right away, Honey, I've got to run into town (meaning Minneapolis). Be back sometime this afternoon."

This precipitated what I shall now characterize as a spirited exchange of viewpoints. A more honest person might have labeled our dialogue a vitriolic argument, ending when I admonished, "You are not to touch the blame thing until I get home! I promise . . . first thing I'll do is read the instruction manual . . ."

"You're gonna read the manual . . . first?" she wailed.

"And what's wrong with that?" I shuddered to think about putting the thing together.

The instruction book I'd perused at the store looked like launch instructions for a moon rocket. I clearly remember thinking: How am I ever going to figure this damn thing out?

"But, Daa ud . . ."

"I mean what I say, Susan. You're not to go near it . . . till I've had a chance to read the instructions."

"But you'll take for-ever!"

"Look, Suze, it's expensive; it's worth the time to be careful with it . . . just too damn complicated to mess with before you know what you're doing."

"But . . ."

"That's the end of it. You don't touch it until I get back. Got it?"

"Yeah."

We finished the ride back home in non-birthday-festive silence. I deposited Sue and her boxes by the back door and offered a final dissuasion. "I'll be home in a while. Don't even think of opening the thing!"

"Yeah."

It was dusk when I returned from my meeting in the city. As I opened the back door, a blast of rock music (cacophony is a better word than music) nearly staggered me. It didn't take Sherlock Holmes to deduce the source.

What could I say? You disobeyed my instructions . . . made your behind-the-times old Dad look like a dope. I said nothing, but played "Ride of the Valkyries" at full volume in my little study, next to her bedroom. After that, we often dueled through the wall. Our choice of weapons—stereo sets.

Sometimes it's best not to beat the obedience drum too loudly. In this instance, there was already enough noise.

obituary—Many of the obituaries that I have read, and recently I read them assiduously, picture the "late lamented" in almost mythic superlatives. From their depictions, I hardly recognize some of my deceased friends—should have shaken hands (maybe even kissed the hem of their garments) more often with some of those departed, fourth-estate legends. Their awesome courage as they "courageously" (favorite word) battled disease, their glorious antecedents, the inconsolable emptiness visited upon bereft survivors, and the inevitable welcoming embrace of the Almighty, prompts me to wonder how I missed all that grandeur. Because I suspect a smattering of hyperbole in these descriptions, I hereby write my own obituary; forgive me, if I attempt to emulate the typical obituary writer's style.

Cranky Curmudgeon Croaks. Sighs of relief swept over the land like a prairie cyclone on reports of the passing of wanna-be composer, writer, and punster, Frederick Blanch. Following a cowardly, panicked flight from cancer, he went to his Maker's arms on— (fill in date from death certificate). It is rumored by many, in religious circles, that aforesaid "Maker" withdrew his arms, precipitating a rather ignominious tumble into obscurity (nice word for Hades). He was preceded in death by Genghis Kahn, George Washington, and Nicola Tesla. He was noted for absolutely no significant accomplishments during a mostly wasted life, during which he frittered away his time scratching out pretend music and useless verse. Neither he nor his stupid puns will be much missed.

old—In the early part of my life it seemed I was never old enough to do what I wanted. Then, for quite a while, I was too old to do what I wanted. As of this writing, I'm just plain too old.

optimist—Mom was an optimist—after birthing me, it was simply a defense mechanism.

P

passive-aggressive — It's my understanding that, currently, the term "passive-aggressive" is no longer listed in the Diagnostic and Statistical Manual as an official title for non-cooperators. If that is so, I suggest a new use for this perfectly good label, now wasting away as a footnote. Bring it out of mothballs, and apply it to the cursing, middle-finger-waving maniacs who roar past old fogy drivers (like me), cruising at less than these impatient folks' desired speed.

patents — I was granted a patent for a lighted advertising display light and I simply cannot remember if the application for a system of dispersing heat (from a solar collector) into a sand bed beneath concrete flooring resulted in an actual patent — it might have. I've often thought of reinventing myself, but could never figure out a satisfactory solution for disposing of the old me.

patience — I learned something about patience from Dad, or at least what patience wasn't. He was at his most "wasn't" during the occasions he tried to tutor me in arithmetic. He was sort of a "Sunday-afternoon" mathematician, if making endless chicken scratches, probably math formulas, in big notebooks indicated being a mathematician. Anyway, Dad couldn't seem to accept the fact that he had produced a kid who thought two and two was a ballet dancer's dress. And speaking of "two," Dad used two schools of teaching technique. Attempting to sharpen my reasoning powers by applying the Socratic method, he would bellow something like, "Are you trying to be an idiot, or are you just plain stupid?" He was pretty clever about combining two questions in one sentence, probably figuring it out in advance in one of those big workbooks. Usually, at that point in our pedagogic adventures, I would be crying and sniveling, and Dad, always on his "teaching toes," would switch instructional approaches, generally to the Attila-the-Hun school of persuasion. "You dumhead!" he would yell, "I ought to give you something to really blubber about!"

I never absorbed much math, but I learned a thing or two — maybe even a thing or two and two — about patience.

perception — Being a peddler, and a bit of a huckster for much of my adult life, I look back and am amazed at my obtuseness; it was not until well past the life begins at . . . milestone that I realized what a powerful tool I had unwittingly wielded as a salesman: perception. It required a herd of Holstein cattle to help me conclude that, in many instances, perception is at least as strong — and occasionally perhaps stronger — than reality. I probably could have skipped the cow thing and learned the same lesson from a five-minute discussion with my friend (and hypnotist) John-Ivan Palmer. But, back to the didactic bovines.

There was a fifteen-year period when I lived in the countryside some five miles south of Annandale, MN. I purchased a couple of farms bordering a small Wright County lake, Slough Lake (one of some nine Minnesota lakes of that name), and built a fancy house (at least by my standards) in the woods. My drive to work in Minneapolis consumed a little more than an hour, and preferring the "back roads" to the highway, I passed many farms during my commute.

Just west of Maple Lake, a particular pasture of some forty acres caught my eye. Surrounded by fields devoted to grain crops, it connected to a distant barn by a narrow lane of perhaps three-quarters of a mile and, though quite desolate and snow-swept in the winter, it quartered about twenty head of Holsteins in the summer. Being a rather slow learner, half of August shed from the calendar, the first year of my twice-daily drive-bys, before I noticed that in the morning the cattle bunched in the shade of the pasture's single tree, which grew at the very eastern edge of the acreage. The old maple had survived, I assume, by virtue of its location on the fence line; it had grown around the strands of barbed wire, burying them deep within its trunk. The tree cast a shadow of irregular shape, which all the cows managed to huddle into. The herd very obviously sought out the shade, for as the shadow shifted according to time and/or day, the cows contrived to stay within its dark confines. Oddly, they contentedly lounged in the very same place in the late afternoon burning sun, when the shade was cast outside of the fence. A dilapidated shed flanking a watering tank did provide enough afternoon shade to accommodate several of the creatures, but in many years of afternoon observations, I never noted a single cow taking advantage of it. I finally concluded that those cows were cooler if they thought they rested in the shady spot. The placebo effect? Perhaps. I choose to think that what one thinks is real, is real, to the thinker—but that's just my perception.

photography—Aunt Katherine (to whom you were introduced in previous pages) would spin in her grave if she knew what a prevaricator (her polite word) she made of me and how I revel in the untruths. I was somewhere around age ten when, at her instigation, I began to develop my own pictures. We moved from Claremont just as I began the third grade, but on a return visit, my wonderful Aunt produced a Sears, Roebuck photo kit she had ordered especially for me—she was an inveterate catalogue shopper—and that began my love affair with photography, a pursuit that nicely dovetailed with an avid interest in the natural kingdom. For a number of years after that, my fingernails sported a yellowish hue and the vinegary smell of stop bath rarely deserted my nostrils. Color film put an end to my darkroom days as its developing requirements were exorbitantly complicated and expensive. Not all downside, however. Color pictures released photography from its dream-like, gray or sepia slavery and replicated the vivid world, reinforcing the (then) familiar adage: pictures don't lie. Before color (BC), a photographer could shoot from odd angles, add or subtract a little light, or sneak in props (like cotton for clouds) to influence the image, but what

Northern Shrike taken by a Kodak "brownie" camera, held at arm's-length (1943)

the camera saw was usually a fairly close match to the end product, and a little light and shadow notwithstanding, good photography was mostly a matter of luck and cropping. Sadly, for the eidetic image, pictorial truth now sleeps with the passenger pigeon and the dodo; photography inevitably followed the Pied Piper of digital electronics, enabling pictures to lie like politicians—and I admit to being the president of photographic Pinocchios.

My earliest efforts to record nature with silver nitrate enlisted the aid of a Kodak box camera, an elegant recorder of fact. An example of the "brownie" camera's simple integrity, a Northern Shrike captured in 1943, righteously displays its gray and black veracity on my office wall among the colorful wonders collected from the jungles and wild places of the world, wonders tweaked and teased by colluding cameras. In addition, I have subjected many of the same exotic photographs to the marvels of computer manipulation in order to produce even more exotic and beau-

tiful lies. Perhaps, being a pretend composer of music has emboldened me to interpret Mother Nature's nearly always perfect compositions of form, texture, and color to my own visual vanities. Though I apologize to my aunt's memory, for I am certain she would find me blasphemous, I find it enormously satisfying to impose my artistic notions on nature via digital legerdemain; it's a little like being the Almighty.

1's and 0's are probably no immediate threat to Monet

poems — see Appendices/Poems, pages 136 to 144.

poet — Most readers should skip this. I blundered onto an original poetic form and called it an Octasym: eight lines, two stanzas, first line, one (of any kind) metered foot; second line, two; third line, three, fourth line, four; fifth line four; sixth line, three, seventh line, two; and eight line, one. It won a first place in a State contest, new forms category. see "Silhouette," etc. Appendix, page 143.

poetry — I will not make the following judgment, though I am tempted: Poetry is a great solipsistic exercise for many contemporary writers, many of whom seem not to have much of a foundation in the art. Nowadays, tortured little lines of prose are often labeled poetry. Much "poetic" outpouring sounds as if the frustrated writer lacks a "dog to kick." Scant attention to the beauty of sound, metaphor, meter, rhyme, or, I assume — effort — is required for its production, resulting in pronouncements of scant consequence. Oh! Mia culpa?

presto — a musical term demonstrated by my grade-school music teachers, who couldn't get through our lessons fast enough.

pride — I have thoroughly enjoyed all seven traditional deadly sins, perhaps even added a few new ones. Most of my transgressions were so numerous that it is difficult to remember specifics, for example, at what meal did I most gluttonously overeat or what was my most lustful moment. However, I do remember the most prideful moment of my life. I was so filled with the sin of pride that I'm sure to become a sizzling prideburger in the hot place.

Sometime in 1994 I received a commission to write a chamber work for a very promising young cellist's "coming out recital;" Bjorn was to be accompanied by his mother, a flutist. My daughter, Susan, accompanied me to the premiere of the work, "Bifröst — Bridge of Rainbows," given at a nice venue (Janet Wallace Music Hall/Macalester College). The six hundred-seat auditorium overflowed, which had nothing to do with my composition, but was, nonetheless, very satisfying to me. I was requested to say a few words preceding the presentation, which I did, and following the concert, the conductor of a local symphony searched me out in the milling crowd and offered congratulations on my "fine piece of music." Accorded such a kudu, in my daughter's presence, made me feel twelve feet tall. She will probably not remember the incident but I will take it to my grave as my greatest sin of pride. The cellist, now professional, is currently a member of the St. Louis Symphony Orchestra.

protector — This little anecdote might have just as appropriately been listed under "champion" or "defender," but protector will suffice. My protector, in this incident, lacked muscle, bulk, or gun-power, but was just as effective as if possessing all three.

I spent the summer of 1945 digging Ribes (gooseberry plants, which harbor pine rust) and fighting forest fires in the Klamath National Forest, which straddles the California-Oregon border. We (teens and some long-term California convicts — most other males were in the armed forces at that time) lived in an encampment of a half-dozen barracks, a mess hall, and an administration building in the mountains north of Yreka, California. I bunked in barracks number two and had limited contact with the residents of the other barracks; in one of those, resided a sizeable group of pre-draft age fellows from San Diego known as "The Italians." For the most part, they were friendly, cooperative, and cheerful. The exception was their largest member, Brutus. He stood well over six feet and was rumored to send weight-scale needles past the three hundred pound mark. He was arrogant, surly, unbelievably mean, and intimidated everyone, even the tough-as-weathered-leather old-timers that led us tenderfeet.

One example illustrates both his social skills and the nexus to me. Our swaying, bouncing, pell-mell transport to forest fires via ancient, open forestry trucks, into which were crammed more bodies than its benches could accommodate, required some to stand. And, even the best of the isolated mountain "roads" we habitually traveled were hardly more than pocked and hummocked deer trails. After pee-call stops, the jostling for seats was even more fierce than our original boarding. However, in spite of the severe stress of a standing ride, a couple of spaces next to Brutus always remained empty. During the rush to a major fire at Horse Creek in mid July, we halted to clear snow that made the road impassable. "The Italians" had never seen snow up close and eagerly volunteered to help shovel an opening. Rather than ask to be allowed to help, Brutus walked up to a boy from Tennessee, yanked the shovel from his hands and knocked the unfortunate lad out cold with the shovel handle. All were aghast, but what could we do?

Perhaps a trifle more vocal in my criticism than the others, I incurred the malevolent attention of Brutus, who cast me a look that Lucrezia Borgia could have used instead of poison. He rode in a different truck, however, and I forgot about him for the next backbreaking week of chopping, scraping duff, and the frenzy of clearing firebreaks.

In camp, after the fire, we were entitled to a couple of days rest. On the first day, I rose early, begged the cook to make me a lunch sandwich, and hiked into the surrounding forest, spending the entire day looking for birds and collecting interesting looking beetles and the like. The next day, after breakfast, I headed back to the barracks, hoping to repeat the previous day's activities. Alone and busy packing my knapsack, a noise caused me to look up; Brutus filled the doorway.

"I get you now, you mouthy little bastard!"

He said no more as he advanced. I've never seen a more menacing, threatening smile. I looked for an escape, but there was only a single, narrow aisle between the rows of bunks –occupied by three hundred pounds of fearsome bully. The only loose thing I could have grabbed for defense was a dirty shirt on an adjacent bunk. Had I snatched it up, I might not be here today; most likely he'd have choked me with it. He was nearly upon me and there was nothing. Nothing! I had no thoughts, just panicked fear as my hand, undirected by any conscious thought, dipped into my shirt pocket and withdrew the matchbox I used to hold collected insects. I pushed the box open and dumped a medium sized *Paruroctonus silvestrii*, a California Common Scorpion, onto my palm. It seemed as surprised as my harasser, its only movement was a waving telson—stinger; for me, it was the cavalry's battle-flag leading a just-in-the- nick-of-time rescue. Brutus froze. His dark face whitened. He whirled and rapidly walked from the barracks. Never again was I treated to his proximity, for which I am eternally grateful to my champion, my defender, my protector.

published—I've been pub-lished but a few times, you know, completely lished from a bit too much time in a pub.

pugilist—I was not allowed to play football in high school. Too small. I deeply resented being relegated to the swimming team where I floundered in mediocrity. Therefore, in my freshman year at the

University of Minnesota, I "went out" for the boxing team. To my surprise, against those more mature war veterans (this was in 1947, following World War II), I flailed to the Championship of the Novice Boxing Tournament, as a lightweight. Most people have considered me pretty much a lightweight ever since, regardless of my maximus belt line.

The boxing Coach, Ray Chisholm, a pug-nosed former fighter, was the referee and I'm not sure if I won on the merits of my performance or Coaches' desire to keep me around, probably the latter. I met Coach on the street some ten years after graduation, and, during our conversation, he mentioned that I was "the hardest working kid" he had ever coached. I'm sure that was code for "no talent," but I enjoyed his assessment more than winning that amateur title.

pun — This is my favorite humor form. If there are punitentiaries in the after-life, I will be punitively punished by some punk punching me until I'm punctured. I don't expect literary pundits to appreciate this puny effort.

quetzal — One of the great privileges in my life was the opportunity to visit the more than mile-high Savegre Valley in Costa Rica and photograph the resplendent quetzal. Few of Nature's creations equal the color and beauty of this feathered wonder.

R

record — Unless it's something like traffic tickets (only a couple, thankfully), I generally keep detailed records of past activities. However, the one record I most would have liked to keep, musical performances, disappeared in the maw of a past computer. On realizing my loss, I set a personal record for creative execration.

regret — Like a castaway on a desert island with a fishbone inextricably stuck in his throat, I cannot disgorge the shame of an oft made, but unkept promise — though a small boy's promise. Both Grandmother and Aunt Katherine longed for fur coats; perhaps no one else knew of their particular desire, but I did. To both, I repeatedly promised, "When I grow up, I'll get you a fur coat," a pledge I did not honor. I could have done so, but, preoccupied with my own pursuits, I never gave that promise a thought until after their deaths. How easy it would have been to give them such a simple pleasure, never mind a pittance of reciprocity for their loving devotion. I should have learned from Khayyám's observation: " . . . having writ . . . Tears [won't] wash out a Word of it."

Of my many regrets, the chief is that I became (Mother would have loved this one) too soon old and too late smart.

rejection — I received more than fifty rejections of Ride without Colors, my fourth novel, from book agents. Note that I do not dignify them as "literary" agents. (Ouch! a tender spot.)

root beer — The family moved from Claremont during the early part of my third grade school year.

Dad got a job with a Minneapolis company, Electric Machinery Mfg. Co. — EM — and was sent to St. Louis. I have many special memories of our two year stay on Tholozan Ave, but will spare the reader and relate but three.

First, about a month after I had been admitted to school, a gang of about ten of my third grade schoolmates beat me up after school. It wasn't a terrible experience; there were so many of them that they beat on each other more than me. Following their assault, the ringleader explained my offence: being from Minnesota.

Secondly, the St. Louis zoo was heaven. Summers, when school was out, Dad would drop me off at the zoo on his way to work and pick me up on his way home. I loved it! However, I certainly wouldn't permit any nine-year-old of mine to spend nine or ten un-supervised hours in that sort of environment. In defense of my parents, it was a more innocent time.

Thirdly: My parents get no defense on this one. If air-condi-tioning was extant in those days, it hadn't made its way to the gen-eral public. On hot, humid nights, St. Louians simply stewed in their own juices. On particularly scorching evenings, we would top off a cooling drive with a visit to one of the numerous A & W root beer stands. Served in chilled, heavy glass mugs, the delicious, foamy brew simultaneously pleasured the taste and cooled parched throats. Without closing my eyes, I can still see the metal tray affixed to the driver's open window, two large mugs and two miniature mugs, their slightly tangy aroma drifting in to my sister and me, in the back seat. Dad would hand back the tiny mugs to us, along with a stern, "Don't spill!"

My sister was somewhat past three years old and took her time daintily consuming the treat. I downed mine in a couple of swallows and asked the usual question, "Am I old enough now . . . to get a big mug?"

"Not yet," was Dad's invariable reply.

It was several years later that I realized why I had never been "old enough" to qualify for a big mug of root beer. The small, chil-dren's mugs were free.

S

salesman—As a pre-school child, I was painfully, almost psychotically, shy (Dad described me as being shy about half a brain). While Dad, Mom, and I still lived with my grandparents, I would run into the orchard or, if trapped within the house, hide beneath a bed whenever visitors, or even family members, stopped by. This persisted until roughly eighth-grade, when I decided that I absolutely had to come out of my shell and face the world. Result: overcompensation—hugely! I sought out opportunities to speak up in school, join clubs, or meet new people. I became a door-to-door *Liberty Magazine* salesman. (About a thousand rejections for each sale hardened my ego's shell almost as much as Dad's constant criticism. Great preparation for a hopeful writer.) About the only serious pursuit in my entire adult life that didn't involve direct selling was a nine month, self imposed, sentence to the "devil's island" (in my opinion) of International Milling Company.

If there is some further place at the end of my present road, I wonder if I'll talk myself in—or out.

separator—The Depression motivated many residents of Claremont to try and economize by providing their own food. I was about six when the family of my closest pal, Sonny Cutler, acquired a cow named Lucrezia; Sonny acquired the task of the second daily milking. He and I were as inseparable as milk and cream, with but two houses separating Grandmother's and Cutlers', and I frequently accompanied him during his late afternoon chore.

Across Front Street, through Mrs. Esketts yard, and over the railroad tracks brought us to Lucrezia's pasture. Usually, she would be waiting at the fence, stoically chewing her cud, but when we were extra late, she chided us by shaking her head sideways and balking when Sonny rubbed her swollen, and probably painful, udder. Generally, her statement made, she fussed no further.

It was a month or so into the Cutler dairy project, as my friend settled on the cut-down old chair used as a milking stool, he proudly announced. "We got us a 'sep-rater.'"

"Gonna pasture it with Lucrezia?"

No, dummy! It ain't uh animal . . . it's uh . . . just wait un I'll show ya, when we finish up here."

Six or seven minutes later Sonny pushed Lucrezi'a flank and she wandered off to graze and make ready for her early morning contribution to the Cutler breakfast table. My friend picked up the two-thirds full pail of warm milk when I impatiently asked, "Hey, what about that 'sep rater' you was gonna tell me about?"

"Okay, Sonny (both of us bore that nickname), I'll show ya." He released his grip on the pail and fumbled with the buttons on his trouser fly. In moments, a yellow stream descended into the bubbling milk. I suppose my face registered not a little surprise; in answer, Sonny said, "It's okay. It's okay! Dad says the sep-rater takes everything outta the milk and puts the cream into uh separate pail . . . everything else just gets dumped."

In the shed behind the Cutler house, I watched Sonny empty the pail into a cast iron and gleaming nickel-plated marvel of technology. "Now, watch this!" He pressed a button on the magenta colored casting. Flywheels spun, the marvel-machine vibrated and hummed. Then, a sloshing stream of snowy liquid cascaded into a large pitcher. "There, just milk," Sonny said, beaming like a magician pulling an unexpected rabbit from his hat. "Didn't I tell ya? Cream's up in that shinny thing on top." What a wonder. And it found its way to Claremont. Another wonder.

Recalling the incident, I'd agree with Sonny's Dad; that machine was truly a separator. I'm not too convinced the machine separated any liquid impurities from Lucrezia's bounty, but I'm pretty sure it separated Sonny's Dad from some of his hard-earned cash.

shoes — If I'm an unredeemable heathen, I place half the blame on uncomfortable shoes.

I indistinctly remember some snow, some school, and some Christmases, but oddly, now that I try to think back, most of my Claremont year's memories are associated with warm weather. I can't explain that; Freud might attribute it to temperature related, penis-size anxiety.

Aunt Katherine taught the first few grades of Sunday School, which, in the summer, I did my best to avoid — for two reasons. First,

I begrudged even a couple of inside hours listening to Biblical stories that Aunt Katherine had already stuffed into me, hours better spent listening to the gurgling song of bob-o-links or the wind whispering through nodding popples. Second, I hated shoes. Sunday School was the only activity, during the entire summer, that required the painful captivity of my calloused, often cut and bruised, but freedom-loving, gloriously bare feet.

Distinctly of another mind, and not much of a negotiator, Dad would, under the banner of righteousness, force my rebellious toes into the confines of shoes that were, probably, a size too small. This operation entailed much wailing and struggling on my part and much yelling and struggling on Dad's part, augmented with much slapping, and even here, Dad righteously observed the Golden Rule: (paraphrased) it is better to give than receive. On that, of course, it was my turn to be of another mind. However, it was matter over mind and Dad had the Almighty on his side.

"By Golly! No kid of mine is going to duck Sunday School." When he deposited me on the steps to the church, the Lord's work was done.

It took only a couple Sundays of tedium and aching feet before, on subsequent days of rest, I arose before the sun. I would spend the morning down at the creek and return home sometime mid-afternoon. The inevitable retribution was no more difficult than that of the capture process, and I had spared myself both boredom and two hours of exquisite foot pain. Though not realizing it at the time, it was a valuable entrepreneurial lesson on net cost.

All costs, however, are not the same. What might I have learned from those missed Sunday School lessons? Might I have become a better person? If so, I blame it on the shoes.

silkscreen printing—I might have mentioned that I'm a little conservative. I picked a business that had, essentially, remained unchanged in several thousand years. That's just my style. But, just my luck, it underwent more change during my tenure with it than in all its history, demonstrating that I'm not a good guesser, a very poor guesser, actually. I invented a machine to silkscreen print T-shirts, but neglected patent application on the grounds that T-shirt printing was just a fad. Brain-power may start the engine, but luck often chooses the road taken.

slap — The word doesn't quite do justice to the assiduous educational endeavors administered by my father. If I irritated him past his "boiling-point," I'd get a smart slap on the side of my head. I gave up trying to figure out if his efforts made me any smarter, it gave me a headache.

slingshot — With some memorable exceptions, fond memories of my father are just about as numerous as the occasions when I won the Irish Sweepstakes. Yet, exceptions there were, and I associate slingshot with one of them.

We lived in the "Weber House" the Christmas I was seven. There, I received one of the greatest gifts for which a small-town, Depression era boy could wish.

Beginning shortly after Thanksgiving, Dad mysteriously spent a number of afternoons in the basement — the earthen cavern beneath the dining room — solely occupied by the furnace. He had expressed his dislike for our personal dungeon many times, so it piqued my interest that he chose to spend time down there. Of course, I tried to see what was happening, but was summarily commanded to "Get back upstairs!" On Christmas morning, I made the connection. There, on the small, trimmed tree, hung my dream: a perfect slingshot. A tag lettered in Dad's ultra-precise lettering simply said, "Sonny."

Dad had selected a perfect Y crotch from an ironwood tree and carved an instrument of superb balance and beauty. The body was honed to just the right finish — had I been less selfishly excited and more observant, I might have found the slight ridges lovingly whittled into the blade resistant material to be a surrogate for my father's unvoiced feelings, but my interest focused on the gift rather than the giver. The sling was cut from an old tire inner-tube and tied to the ends of the body with such precision that the ends of the string were invisible.

My gratitude, "Gosh! Thanks, Dad!" was boundless, but ephemeral.

Winter presented inanimate targets such as old soup cans and snowmen. However, by spring, I had acquired enough skill to terrorize nearly all of Claremont's birds, cats, dogs, and chipmunks, a skill I now regret. But, regret tempered by the memory of Dad's afternoons spent in our dungeon, creating the perfect gift for me. I'll say it with sincerity this time: gosh! thanks, Dad.

small-town — My hometown, Claremont, is the quintessential exemplar. Small geographically, it confined a small population, and when I resided there, not a few Claremont-sized minds.

spelling — This is one of those silly conventions that my English teachers used to berate me about. Silly conventions like never ending sentences with a preposition or leaving them incomplete. Ever recalcitrant, I have successfully resisted their indoctrination. My opinion is: if a writer can't spell a word more than one way it indicates a lack of imagination — he/she should get out of the business. Perhaps that's why I've never really gotten into the business.

succinct — I really do not have sufficient space to do complete justice to the definition of this word; suffice it to say, that as an author of crisply efficient and pithy prose, I abhor verbosity — nor do I favor nounnosity, adjectivosity, or adverbosity.

super-sonic — The cosmic speed at which money seems to linger with me. Einstein should have checked my wallet before making silly assertions that nothing can exceed the speed of light.

sweet rolls — Alice Hinkley's Front Street house was across the road from Grandma's. Her husband, Dana, published The Claremont News in a tiny building that, today, couldn't accommodate a Ford Sedan. The Claremont gossip mill linked Dana with his assistant, Adelade, but I don't think there was room enough in the little printing establishment to sneeze, let alone host romantic assignations — certainly not in comfort. Nevertheless, I don't think Dana spent much time at home, which left Alice with lots of time on her hands — wondrously skilled hands, crafting bakery fit for mythic beings. Fortunately, in little backwater Claremont, the gods had overlooked Alice and her incomparable pastry, permitting us mortals to revel in her Olympian fare. A boyhood pal, Sonny Cutler, and I would show up for samples, and stay for "seconds" and "thirds." Generous Alice, and her heavenly sweet rolls, never disappointed us.

T

talkative — Mother lived by a large number of platitudinous aphorisms. One of her favorites was, "children should be seen and not heard." Another was, "do as I say, not as I do," this was more applicable to me than the first. Though she constantly counseled me to "shut up," I was, nonetheless, voted the "most talkative" person in my senior high school class. In discussing this dubious complimentary laurel with my mother, she confided that she also had been accorded that distinction on her graduating class's "Roll of Fame." At my daughter Susan's high school graduation ceremonies, the back of the graduation program displayed the sketch of a plaque with names of students noted as "most likely to succeed," "best dancer," etc. Awarded the honor of "most talkative," was the latest of our lineage to uphold that noble appellation: blabbermouth.

I wonder if Mom ever stopped to think how the publication of this family weakness reconciled with her very favorite clichéd adage: "fools' names and fools' faces are often seen in public places."

taste — Out-of-step with mainstream tastes was not intentional; it just happened, like green eyes and left-handedness. I often wished I could enjoy pop music, golf, current celebrities, and other public fascinations, so I might better "fit in," but the "three B's" enchanted my ears, the natural world my eyes, and special admiration for my fellows mostly limited to those contributing something of lasting value to society, like Nikola Tesla — I don't care that he was a little goofy.

Sometime around senior high school graduation, I wrote a verse lamenting this nonconformity. I recall nothing but the final lines:

"The whole world seems . . . sweet milk chocolate and jazz, While I am bittersweet and Bruckner."

teacher — I served a ten year stint as a once a week, evening instructor, which required a license and teaching certificate. When I sold my printing and associated businesses, Northwest Technical College (now operating under a more prestigious name) approached me to design and teach a weekly, nighttime course for adults, "Going into Business." I accepted, as a means of giving something back to the capitalistic system.

During my tenure, the stock market experienced a precipitous fall, on a class day, just as we were addressing how stock is theoretically valued. Using Target Stores stock as an example, I explained that, though its stock's price had fallen by fifty percent (from some forty plus dollars to about twenty dollars a share) its intrinsic value had not, the Company had no less inventory, not a penny less cash on hand, and retained the same capital assets as before the crash. "It will surely rise to pre-crash levels," I asserted, "buy their stock tomorrow and make yourselves some money." The following week, at class time, Target stock was right back to its pre-crash price, yet, not one of my students had taken my advice to double their money; that makes me a lousy teacher.

television — I was a university student when first exposed to what most folks considered the eighth wonder of the world: television. A friend held a party during a Minnesota Gopher football game and treated our assemblage to the game on the TV. Housed in a cabinet the size of a Buick, the screen was about the size of a stunted grapefruit. The picture fluttered, faded from "snow," and suffered violent electronic nystagmus, but we thought it an absolute miracle.

I never dreamed that some day I'd produce 140 regular TV shows (plus a few non-scheduled productions), one of which was named the best arts show on public TV in 1995. As I was utterly debilitated by Meniere's Syndrome at that time, Barbara Nolan (NWCT Public Access Manager) picked up the award for me, in Boston. I am relieved to be free from the pressures of production, but very much miss our crew and the interesting guest musicians.

tool — Lately, when I think of the word tool, it's likely precipitated by television pictures of a chimpanzee dipping sticks into an ant hill — a clever creature using tools. I greatly admire skilled tool wielders, carpenters, auto mechanics, and others — like dentists.

Dentists use a veritable arsenal of unusual tools: scalers, excavators, evacuators, curettes, elbows . . . elbows? You betcha! I might even owe the intact roof of my mouth to a dental surgeon's elbow.

It began as I held my mouth open for Bruce's inspection. Not only my dentist, Bruce was a landlord/friend of sorts, permitting me to keep forty or so bee colonies in his alfalfa fields near the Becker, Minnesota power plant. It was a tradeoff; my bees pollinated his hay crop and I got the honey.

"This is not good," he said.

"Uh . . . uh."

"You've got to get these gums pared back . . . way too high."

I didn't like his use of the words pared and gums in one sentence. Didn't pared indicate some sort of blade? As he removed his tools, hands, and other equipment from my mouth, I blurted, "You mean you want to cut on my gums?"

"I'm not going to do it . . . takes a specialist. It's not a big deal. Harold . . . friend of mine . . . oral surgeon, one smart cookie."

"I'd like to think it over."

"What's to think about? You want your own teeth don't you?" Bruce didn't wait for an answer. "You might need more than one appointment . . . usually does a gingivectomy . . . uppers and lowers separately. We'll make the first appointment for you."

Bruce's nurse entered the room a few minutes later and gave me a date. "That's 1:30 sharp," she emphasized sharp, "they don't like late show-er uppers."

And that's how I was shanghaied into a ginger-what-uh-me.

I arrived at the dental surgeon's office on the appointed day with ten minutes to spare. Nonetheless, it was a half-hour before the receptionist ushered me into a typical dentist's room: articulating chair, instrument tray, water basin, etc. Untypically, a large television set blared from a sturdy looking metal bracket attached high on the wall in front of the operating chair.

A young woman in white, whom I assumed to be a dental assistant, sat on a low, wheeled stool, fixated on the television. She radiated eye watering, overpowering perfume, enough to cause green plant destruction for a block in all directions. A black streak, as wide as my hand, separated long blonde tresses splaying over her shoulders. She chewed a large wad of gum with the vigor (but not the stealth) of a spy trying to swallow secret evidence.

Without removing her gaze from the television set, she advised me to, "Sit yerself down . . . with ya in uh shake."

I sat as instructed. The hygienist ignored me for several minutes — until the program that held her attention concluded. I struggled to be non-judgmental. Perhaps her furious mastication was some therapeutic tooth thing. Maybe she simply stalled to cover for the still absent surgeon. However, I couldn't rid the notion that she'd be more at home dancing on a bar than wilting the dieffenbachia in a doctor's office. I was jolted from my unkind reverie.

"Hey, Harold! . . . It's over," she called in a voice obviously calculated to penetrate closed doors.

The doctor entered and addressed his assistant. "We can turn it off now, Heidi." As an afterthought, he added the last words he would ever utter to me, "Nice to make your acquaintance, Mr. Blanch . . . let's get right to it."

Getting "right to it" began with about four, very painful shots of Novocain into my upper jaw, followed by a short disappearance of the doctor, and then after his return a considerable amount of crunching, sucking away blood and tissue, and finally, coating the open wounds with a clay-like material. Doctor Harold spoke not a word during the entire procedure. I concluded that he finished when the scalpel clattered onto the instrument tray and he left the room.

This was Bruce's friend; what did he see in the guy? He had a personality identical to a rock I once tripped over, bloodying my knee. No, as I recall, the rock was more sympathetic.

"I do the clean-ups," said his assistant, now decorated with red smears of my blood. "Gladys uhl make an appointment for ya . . . ya know . . . lowers."

It took a brave man or a fool to go a second round with Harold and Heidi, and I am not a brave man.

Ten day later, I was back. This time, at 1:00. As the World Turns, or whatever the soap-opera was, had just begun. Anesthetic injections into the lower jaw proved to be more painful than before and slower to take effect. The doctor left the room for five or six minutes while my jaw numbed. All that time, Heidi kept her eyes glued to the TV screen.

Finally, the surgeon returned and round two began in earnest.

Novocain suppressed the pain, did nothing to reduce the frightful wrenching, and amplified the crunching and surging, staccato sucking sounds. I wished that I had something else to think about. Ah-ha! That was the purpose of the television: diversion. From my prone position, I did my best to focus on the screen. From the corner of my eye, I saw that I was not the only viewer; Heidi never even glanced toward the locus of the procedure, yet the suction wand seemed to effortlessly glide around my mouth, picking up fluids and debrided flesh.

Suddenly, the cathode-tube lover slapped his paramour; the actress screamed. I felt a stab of pain in the roof of my mouth.

"Uhg . . . uh, uh." I squirmed in the chair. I swung my head aside. Dr. Harold withdrew his scalpel, but the pain still shot up through my nostrils. Heidi had thrust the suction device into the opening to my nasal cavity and the tool pulled inexorably. Heidi held her gaze on the TV screen as Dr. Harold placed a restraining hand on her arm. My face felt as if it was hosting a nest of hornets at stinging practice.

The doctor's staying hand did not alert the hygienist that her patient pained and her employer wished her attention. All of this happened in just seconds, and as I raised my hand to push the offending tool away, Doctor Harold jabbed Heidi in the side with a vicious swipe of his elbow.

"Ow!" She wailed, then screamed, "Jesus, Harold! What the hell ya doin'?"

In a moment, Gladys, the receptionist, opened the door, glowered at Heidi, and asked, "Is everything alright, Doctor?" Doctor Harold pointed to the television set. Gladys reached up, turned it off, and eased the door closed as she left. I heard her say, I suppose to those in the waiting room, "Just a little problem with the TV volume."

I had raised up and bent to the little gurgling drain, coughing and spiting scarlet into its pearlescent porcelain throat.

Doctor Harold remained silent. He gently grasped the suction wand, held it in front of Heidi's eyes for a moment, and replaced it in her hand.

The procedure finished smoothly. Ten minutes later, I was driving home. Besides my aching teeth, the roof of my mouth was a little sore for a couple of days; I survived with but a single phobia. No, not of dentists, but of Minneapolis nightspots. I avoided them for long afterward—for fear of running into Heidi dancing on the bar.

Eventually, however, just the memory remained that Bruce was right. It took "one smart cookie" to improvise a dental instrument in the middle of an emergency; I guess one man's anatomy is another man's tool.

toot My musical interests might indicate that "toot" should connote some sort of horn. Not so. The word conjures up a week of missed classes, the boredom of endless waiting, and pain—extreme pain—indelibly branding "toot" into my psyche.

It was a brush with what, I assume, socialized medicine might resemble. For six days I sat on hard wooden benches of every style, each maliciously designed to render one's backsides completely numb, in hallways teeming with nurses, doctors, and eager medical students. My nose, the victim of a "roundhouse" right hook, lay nestled to my right cheek; I must have looked like a fugitive from a circus sideshow. Nevertheless, countless passing medical students poked, stroked, prodded, and pinched my pain wracked proboscis, most asking if it had not always clung to my cheek ("No, it's always been straight out in front of me."), but none moving to help relieve my obvious misery.

A more adventuresome boy might have demanded immediate attention; however, schooled in complete obedience to authority, I sat and waited because that was my original instruction. But Lady Luck sometimes smiles on tongue-tied lads; in this instance, she brought a friend: I think his name was Dr. Tangen. He was a nose and throat specialist, in private practice in downtown Minneapolis, who taught some classes at the University. He passed by me many times and, finally, asked why I had been sitting for so long, outside his classroom. When I related my circumstances, he went directly to a nearby nurses' station and called his office, canceling his appointments. He then came to me and said, "Come on, no more waiting."

Ushered into a small room, its medical equipment consisting of no more than a rectangular table with stirrups and a fancy chair with a tray attachment, resembling a dentist's chair, the doctor directed me to be seated. Magically—I'm still at a loss for how they materialized—half a dozen or so medical students immediately crowded into the room and ringed the operating chair.

As though I wasn't there, the doctor spoke to his students and, in terms that I could mostly follow, meticulously described each step of the procedure concurrent with its application.

"This will not only anesthetize the patient, you'll note that he will briefly lose consciousness."

The chair-side tray held a small brown bottle, several slender, silver rods, other rods that looked exactly like broom wisps, a jar of white material, a wad of cotton, and an instrument that might be mistaken for an overgrown butter knife.

After removing the bottle-top and pouring some of the jar's contents onto a little paper square, the doctor picked up one of the broom straws. "We'll use two straws and one stainless in each nostril. Note how tightly I roll the cotton on the tip." He deftly twisted cotton on the end of a wisp, making it look like a foot-long Q-tip®.

"Now, we dip the swab into the adrenaline and roll it in the cocaine crystals . . . insert, like this . . ."

Pain, so excruciating that I nearly choked, scorched my head. I wanted to scream but the presence of the students shamed me into silence. The next insertion was no less frightful. Nor the next, and the next, and the next, and the next. I clutched at the arms of the chair—it may as well have been an inquisition rack—and twisted in agony.

"The patient will temporarily lo . . ."

Mercifully, anesthetized, I blacked out. My next recollection is standing and being led to the table. There, the doctor gripped my head in a one-armed headlock that would do a professional wrestler proud and, with the fat butter-knife, proceeded to re-break the mal-healing nasal bones and lever them back into place. I experienced no pain. However, the awful, grinding crunches and the pulling, pushing pressures would have satisfied the most jaded masochist.

Yet, I am eternally grateful to the kindly doctor. Were it not for his solicitude, I might still be waiting on one of those damnably hard Student Health Service benches.

But, back to the relevance of toot, and the nose not nimble enough to dodge adversity.

The training facilities for several minor sports, boxing among them, were closeted beneath the seats, at the extremity of the northwest leg of Minnesota's Memorial football stadium (since razed), then affectionately known as the "Brick House." During a sparring session, I received a smart blow that dramatically rearranged my facial features. Coach stopped the match and gave me directions to Cook Hall, the large building at the open end of the stadium horseshoe housing the swimming and football facilities. We could access it from our training rooms by descending a dimly illuminated stair well and traversing an even darker series of tunnels.

I was directed to report to Lloyd Stein, the famed athletic trainer (for fifty yrs.) during the reins of coaches such as Bernie Berman and Murray Warmath, and the "glory-days" football teams, when Minnesota basked in number one status. I found the trainer in the corner of a huge room filled with Whirlpool baths, rubdown tables, and medical facilities; it smelled like an old sock, a very old sock after a ten-mile hike through a tropic swamp.

Trainer Stein motioned me to the worn, ladder-back chair beside his ancient wooden desk; I sat in a throne hallowed by All-American athletes and humbled by nobodies like myself, but alike in kindred misery. A meaty hand grasped my chin and, with surprising gentleness, turned it at various angles. The stubby fingers released their grip, picked up a pencil, and scribbled "distorted septum LS" on a small pad. As he probably had done more than a thousand times before, the trainer tore off the scrap describing the injury while admonishing, "Student Health Service . . . was you, I'd get my butt there first thing tomorrow morning." He again cupped my chin in his hand and stared a moment before delivering his personal diagnosis, "Umm, ya picked up uh first class toot in the bugle."

travel — If not for Motoko, I might never have rekindled my passion for photography. Stimulated by her desire that we travel to unfamiliar places, the urge to record new wonders became irresistible. I owe her many thanks for reopening the photographic door.

turndown — This anecdote might have been listed under "rejection" or "double jeopardy" or "déjà vu - all over again." However, turndown connotes a negativity that I think appropriate to this story.

In the waning years of the 1960s, I drew up plans for what was for me an ambitious home, to be built on a many acre parcel of wooded property in Wright County (which, at the time, was very rural). It was a labor-of-love and I spent scores of enjoyable hours drawing, erasing, and drawing. I then submitted the plans to a professional architect for technically proper drawings, readable to a building contractor.

The architect undertook, on his own, to completely re-design the home. From its hilltop site, he informed me the new design looked absolutely "regal to a viewer approaching from below." Quite a little tussle ensued between the professional's "artistic expertise" and my "ignorance" of design. The matter was finally settled when I patiently explained that I would not be living in the brush outside, not looking up at his beautiful rendition of the house while I clutched a blanket about my freezing body, but inside the structure, where I didn't care a feather about what others thought of the design. He finally acceded to my vision when I threatened to seek a rival architect. Incidentally, we loved the home as originally laid out, its convenience and livability, and, to my knowledge, no one ever experienced protracted nausea upon viewing its exterior.

The plans were submitted to several contractors, and following as rigorous a vetting process as I could, a builder was tentatively chosen.

I had saved enough cash to pay just over half the cost and sought to finance the other half through a traditional home lender. I avoided my own bank, with which I had excellent relations, wishing not to mix my business affairs with personal financing. Most lenders looked at the plans and said, "Where?" in a tone that indicated this woodlot must be someplace beyond the Sahara desert. One banker, quite taken with his own sense of humor, smiled and said, "We're not licensed for business in Shangri-La." The Farmers and Mechanics Bank, with whom I had saved pennies, as a child, sent their most senior appraiser to actually look at the property. He telephoned me at my office and, in an incredulous but respectful voice, inquired if I had actually seen the property. I assured him that, not only had I walked it a hundred times, I had erected a fence that all bidding contractors had agreed to build within and not harm a blade or twig outside.

"But it's . . . it's way out in the country!" He made the word country sound like a scatological expletive. He ended the conversation with a mumbled rejection and, ". . . Nice homes just aren't built out there . . . in a woods."

Silly me, I had mistaken the yurts in the area for homes.

Plowing ahead, in spite of my obvious ignorance of what species of houses should be built where, I bundled up my plans and contractor's preliminary bids and plopped them on my attorney's desk. Roger, my long-time lawyer, who had begun practice about the same time as I started my business, was now a major partner in a large, successful firm and turned over my building-contract project to a junior lawyer, Ralph.

In due course, a sixty-page draft of the building contract showed up in the mail. I spent several hours changing, adding, deleting, and made another appointment with Roger. He accepted the amended document and I assumed that I'd soon get a final copy. Ralph was present when the "final" contract was handed to me and I glanced through it hurriedly — Roger's billing time was expensive and every minute in his office meant less money in my wallet. Nonetheless, I searched and re-searched for a crucial clause that I had added to the first draft.

"Where's the attorney's fees for a defaulted party, Ralph?"

"Oh, I didn't put that in."

"I've asked for that in every contract you've ever done for me," (perhaps fifty).

Roger seemed to twist uncomfortably in his chair. He knew that I required that clause in any contract and its omission in this one indicated, dare I say, a "sloppy," perusal of his junior's work.

"But, I particularly added it to the draft." Unfortunately, I am guilty of argumentative stridency and, no doubt, I exercised that shortcoming.

In a voice, just slightly condescending, Ralph said, "But it's not standard procedure . . ." I interrupted. "Are you writing the contract for me, or Mr. Standard Procedure? . . . Please, Ralph, just insert that clause!" I'm sure that little bit of sarcasm helped boost my bill; after all, I was just a dumb-cluck layperson with a lot of nerve to meddle in sacrosanct legalese. I was reminded of a sign posted in a Maple Lake, Minnesota, lumber yard: "Labor: $3/hour; If you watch, $5/hour; If you help, $10/hour," but I wasn't about to lose another bicycle on this deal.

As luck would have it, that particular clause saved my financial gizzard, as the entire basement concrete floor, nearly four thousand square feet, had to be jack-hammered up, removed and replaced, and one corner of the home was built without internal support. The private building inspector that was brought on board pointed out numerous other deficiencies requiring extensive rebuilding, all resisted by the contractor, leading to lots of legal arm wrestling. Of course, all the sub contractors got involved. There was a huge meeting of builders and subs, each accompanied by their respective lawyers, where I was exposed as an unreasonable monster for insisting basement drains be functional and second-story walls supported. Nonetheless, that little "fault-plus-attorney's fees" clause stuck.

During this process, Ralph contacted me and asked if I had yet obtained financing.

"No, not yet."

"We're attorneys for the Farmer's and Mechanic's Bank . . . we'd get brownie-points if you'd let me recommend a project like yours . . . I'm on good personal terms with their attorney."

I explained that F & M had already nixed my loan, but Ralph wanted a chance to run it by them again. I had no objection, and he arranged another site appraisal.

No phone call this time. F & M's Senior Appraiser, accompanied by an assistant carrying his boss's brief case and a box wrapped in gift paper, appeared in my office. "Our Chief Counsel requested that we revisit your Wright County property to make a final determination on your loan application." Without much evident regret, the appraiser continued, "I really regret that we will have to deny the application again . . . just can't fit it in our guidelines." Before I could reply, the assistant proffered the fancy box to me, as his superior said, "Note that the card is signed by our President."

Oh, my gosh! A consolation prize . . . and a card—signed by the President! The box contained six, very ordinary water glasses with raised gold embellishments—a picture of the front of the F & M Bank building. In the face of such tangible contrition over their inability to squeeze me into their guidelines, I was speechless. So, I said nothing.

That afternoon I visited my regular bank, Northwestern National Bank (a major fire and several name permutations ago), walked into the Executive VP's office and said, "Pat, I need a pretty hefty loan to finish my house."

"Sure. You want the check this afternoon?"

I ask myself, why do my projects always seem to have to be done twice? Is it karma? Maybe it's that darn Gemini thing I don't believe in.

uncle — see **horse** and **dedication**

unfinished business — Dad succumbed, so the death certificate noted, to congestive heart failure, and he took a long time doing it. For his last several months, he grew ever weaker until it tired him to walk across a room. I made numerous peace overtures, attempts to say goodbye, but he brushed them away; "There's nothing wrong with me!"

He was an intransigent man who, I believe, thought himself several cuts above most of humanity. Therefore, whatever he decided must be right. For example, when the dentist told him he needed treatment for gum disease, he quit the dentist cold. "I don't have gum disease . . . the man's a fool!" He never saw a dentist again. Experience probably justified that attitude; he was not just good at most endeavors, he was exceptional. At one of his company's picnics, I hoped to humiliate him by signing him up for the one-handed soft ball game, mostly played by gorillas impersonating men. He tried to wiggle out, but there I was, in front of a big group of his associates, saying, "Go ahead, Dad, show um how to do it." I was sure he'd get me later, but it would be worth it, to see the world's smartest man take some "humble crow." When he came to bat, he looked diminutive and out of place alongside his muscled teammates, until he hit the ball so far outside the fence it couldn't be found. A brilliant man with an astronomical IQ, he never had chicken pox or mumps or any other childhood malady like the rest of us mortals, nor, remarkably, did he feel regular pain — perhaps he was a cut above.

However, in the relationship department, to me, he was zero. At the end, I wanted to tell him that, "In spite of our differences, there's much I admire about you and I just naturally love you because you're my Dad. Could I just hug you and say goodbye?" But, Dad was having none of that kind of sissy talk.

"There's nothing to 'patch up,' besides, I've told you a hundred times, I'm fine!" He died three days later.

Selfishly, I suppose, I wanted to remember reconciliation and love; sadly, I mostly remember blows and distance. The relationship to my father will forever remain unfinished business.

unsuccessful — A succinct description of my book-writing career.

vacuous — The mind of the editor who cancelled my "humor" column because he thought the country readers might not understand it. The straw that broke his camel brain was a column in which I alluded to a visit to the St. Paul sewage processing plant as an "offal experience."

value — Most of us suffer worthless experiences, other experiences are worthy of suffering.

Mother took me to the dentist when I was twelve; the doctor found several dental caries. Preambled by several examinatory ummms and an aha, the dentist withdrew a hideously sharp pick from my mouth and addressed Mother, "Would you like Novocain, Mrs. Blanch?"

I cowered in the dental chair, heart pounding, mentally beaming images of a pathetic, pain-wracked child, but Mom's telepathic image receiver was on hold as she mulled the question; she responded obliquely, "How much is it?"

"Two dollars."

Mother's decision was scrupulously logical. She replied, "I don't think I need it."

verse — A submission to the now defunct Twin Cities "slick" magazine was rejected by a fledgling editor as "nice verse, but not quite a poem," which you may judge for yourself — see "A Child's Ear," Appendices, page 136.

At the time, I was unhappy with the editor, but upon reflection, I'm quite comfortable any time my scribbling is labeled "nice" anything.

walnut — I have a collection of walnut plaques, some carrying cheap brass plates, some decorated with fancy bronze castings, and some engraved. These awards of "distinction," "merit," "winning," or what-have-you are just cumbersome dust catchers. I think their practical value lies in hanging them over holes in the wall, but when I've encountered folks with a slew of these "grown-up-merit-badges," I've noticed they don't seem to have walls with holes — it's a topsy-turvy world.

warming — I hope I'll never (there's that word I should never use) be accused of ignoring the planet's problems; I won't, if someone would just produce my musical comedy: Global Warming. I'll spare the summary, but mention that a sample song, "A Little Sin," is included in the Appendix, page134.

workaholic — I am and was a card-carrying, certifiably-incurable, workaholic. This, in spite of my parent's (especially my father's) years-long mantra of "you're the laziest kid I've ever seen." Oddly, I was also the "dumbest," "most irresponsible," "ungrateful kid" they had ever seen. I was middle-aged before I realized that my obsessive work habits were simply a manifestation of Newton's third law of motion: "for every action there is an equal and opposite reaction." For whatever modest successes I have blundered into, thanks, Dad.

writer — My first venture at authorship was assisted by Grandpa's old Underwood and abetted by Grandma.

I had importuned my grandmother to allow me the use of Grandpa's typewriter. While I tentatively pressed the keys, adjusting the pressure of the stroke to produce legibility, Grandma sat in the living room, around the corner from the office/parlor, probably entreating Higher Powers to spare Grandpa's writing machine from the unpredictable fingers of her six-year-old grandchild.

I recall rolling in several sheets of paper and pecking a few type characters on each. My crowning achievement, however, was the title to my opus: *The Adventures of the Duo*. I guess it was a mystery story because the plot, the *Duo*, the cast of supporting characters, and the undoubtedly fascinating dénouement will forever remain a mystery, as the title composed the totality of my first literary composition.

Ever since then, I've been driven to commit my fantasies to paper; perhaps the most optimistic of those fantasies is that I am a writer.

x-ray—More than a "snap-shot," but less than a regular autobiography, this insubstantial chapbook x-rays the bones of my life while permitting me the privacy of some unrecorded flesh. Miser-like, I will not share some of my most precious memories. It is sufficient to mention their existence, and that they will surely accompany me on the next leg of my journey.

yellow bird — Birds' beauty and voice have fascinated me throughout eight decades. And, now that memory fades, the mind's eye and ear can accurately recall but a few of the most brilliantly feathered and even fewer avian melodies. However, I hear one particular yellow bird as though sitting before it now — in spite of nearly forty intervening years.

The first Christmas season that we lived in the Annandale School District, my wife and I attended a holiday program featuring the grade school choir. The sixty or so voices included Susan's. She was barely visible among the sea of small faces, from our vantage about halfway back in the large auditorium. Midway through the recital, a slight but incredibly lovely voice singing Yellow bird, Up high in banana tree, floated over the assemblage. We craned to see the owner of the exquisite voice. What child could sing so beautifully? I was astounded to see that my daughter was the soloist, she had not mentioned a word of her part, to us.

Since then, Susan has sung, danced, and acted in innumerable theatric productions, many of which I cannot clearly recall, but "yellow bird" still sings in my memory, undiminished.

you "betcha" — This was tedious work. If you were bored (and got this far), please sympathize a little with the writer. I had to go through all the boredoms, not only a second, but a third and on-and-on ad nauseam times, conflicted by trying for truth, while simultaneously attempting to appear better than I am (or was).

Z

zigzag — Webster's II New College Dictionary defines zigzag as "Something having the shape of a series of sharp turns, . . ." For me, even though operating mostly within the big lump of the bell-curve, that pretty much sums up my life.

Only good fortune has prevented catastrophe on some of those sharp turns, but I suspect the next one could be fatal.

Appendix #1
Acknowledgements

I am definitely not a self-made man. As malleable clay, family members, Zeitgeist, and happenstance shaped my cup of being. And, though that vessel is presently worn and cracked, it is still held intact by many of the hands that participated in its firing.

Jerry Franksen, insurance supervisor/salesman, instructed through both word and industry that today's problems, if tackled often enough, may likely be tomorrow's manageable process.

D.J. Willis, retired entrepreneur, shared from his lifetime's accumulation of business lore.

Some Muses hang around for quite a while. I was fifty when music teacher, Opal Mathson Fisher, fanned a spark of musical interest into a ten-year blaze of creativity. It is difficult for me to separate gratitude for her encouragement from other emotions. This dear person had absolutely no inkling of the warmth of my sentiments. She shares a place in my psyche that is reserved for very special friends.

It's nice to think one's work is appreciated. On many occasions, when I telephoned my great friend, Roman Dicaire, I would hear my music playing in the background—what an ego boost! Thank you, Roman.

Institutions are due some mention too, chief among them, the Minnesota Composers Forum (before it morphed into the American Composers Forum) and Northwest Community Television of Brooklyn Park, Minnesota.

In the writing arena, I am grateful for writing criticism from Maureen Taube LaJoy, who, until her untimely death, became a cherished part of my personal life. I am also indebted to scores of Minneapolis Writers' Workshop members for twenty-five years of writing ambience and critique, especially Herbert Montgomery, P.J. Doyle, Rex Pickett, and John-Ivan Palmer. In particular, I thank Workshop colleague Barbara Grengs, English teacher, author, and mentor, who culled this little opus for screamers.

A chance meeting with Ralph Bauer, in a piano showroom, led to the finalization of a fifteen-year stint as the Director of a non-profit music organization and producer of the Music da Camera television program (for which Yamaha, at Ralph's instigation, provided pianos). However, neither the non-profit nor the television program would have prospered without the considerable assistance of Don Moon Park and Barbara Nolan Clark. Thanks also to Bill Arden, Joyce K. Larson, Mark and Marshalleen Patten, Dick Erickson, and the entire TV crew. To say that I owe my life to the above people sounds melodramatic, but I surely owe each a portion of it. Thank you, my friends.

Lastly, but surely not least, I wish to recognize the couple hundred or more musicians who toiled through the vicissitudes of my musical efforts; they are due my sincere gratitude. I'd like to especially single out:

Adriana Ransom, for an outstandingly beautiful cello performance of both cello/piano pieces, "Solveg's Song" and "Nostalgique."

Victoria Ebel-Sabo. "Bittersweet" has been performed many times, but your exquisite piano interpretation (as I hoped it might be realized) lives as one of my most cherished musical memories.

Thank you for these high-notes!

Appendix #2
Lyrics & Poems

My conception of lyrics differs from poetry in that lyrics should fit musical sound, while poetry, though incorporating sound as integral, conforms to meter and rhyme. A couple of song lyrics follow:

> Just a Little Sin
> Minnesota Tango

I perceive poems to be akin to music in that some might be classified on a scale from "ditties" to symphonies, some as "pop' and some as serious. I have written my share of inconsequential doggerel but, hopefully, a symphony or two (like "Beware the Dogs"—book length poem).

Some of the included poems relate to various "word" entries in *Last Words* or chosen because they could be fitted onto a single manuscript page. I have deliberately placed "Whispers" as the final page of this little book to remind myself that my scribbling posits are not to be taken too seriously.

Following are:

> A Child's Ear
> Unsung Heroes
> A Jar of Petals
> The Loving Cup
> Requiem for a Flower
> Metaphor
> Silhouette
> Gemini, Jekyll, or Janus?
> Whispers

Just a Little Sin

Just — a little sin —
Will — get you in. —
It's like — a ticket —
To — this nice warm place.

There's no hassle here —
With pearly gates. — Upstairs,
We hear — it's crowded.
Hear — there's always space.

Transgressions here,
Are not reviled.
Peccadilloes are,
In vogue.

I ni — qui — ty — & vice —
Are fine. —
Oh how we looove,
A frightful rogue.

Sac — ri — lege —
And — villany —
Will always be —
In style.

Down here —
We see — as nice —
All forms,
Of wicked guile.

So just — a little sin —
Will — get you in. —
It's like a ticket —
That is freeee,

The only price —
A little vice,
A murder — maybe,
Or grand larceny.

Transgressions here,
Are not reviled.
Peccadilloes are,
In vogue.

Ini - qui - ty - & - vice
Are fine. —
Oh how we looove,
A frightful rogue.

Oh how we looooove,
A frightful rogue.

Frederick Blanch

Minnesota Tango

Oh when the winds go blow
And bring the cold and snow,
You know it's time to go —
And do the Minnesota – Tang-go.

Now it isn't very nice.
To live beneath the ice,
So you – will have – to do –
The Minnesota – Tang-go.

I caramba– and oi vey!
(And Uffda too!)
It's another snowy day.
That's status quo –
You'll have to go –
And do the Minnesota – Tang-go.

So forget the grass is gone,
That there's glaciers on your lawn,
Just do – what Minnesotans do –
The Minnesota – Tang-go.

Yes, there's a reason why,
We have June and July.
It's so – the snow can go.
(You can forget for just a while.)
The Minnesota – Tang-go.

Oh when the winds go blow
And bring the cols and snow,
You know it's time to go —
And do the Minnesota – Tang-go.

So put on your caps with flaps,
Your underwear with traps,
(Dress like an Es-ki-moooo)
For you – will have – to go –
And do the Minnesota – Tang-go.

Don your boots, your scarf,
Your gloves well,
And don't – forget – your shov-el.
(Shovel? – Shovel, shovel shovel:)
The Minnesota – Tang-go.

So leave your stately mansions,
Your ramblers or your hovels,
March to the boreal battle
With an army of snow shovel,

For when the winds go blow
And bring the cold and snow,
You know it's time to go —
And do the Minnesota – Tang-go.

Yet snow's not ca-tas-tro-phe,
It promotes de-moc-ra-cy,
For no color nor no creed,
Is exempted from the need,
To do the Minnesota – Tang-go.

Oh when the winds go blow
And bring the cold and snow,
You know it's time to go —
And do the Minnesota – Tang-go.

135

A Child's Ear

When I was young
The wind bore song
To trees and hawks
And I could hear
The words and even
Help a little with the tune.

With artless zest,
I sang along
In happy choir
With new-plowed earth
And lodging grasses,
Crickets, stars, and sun and moon.

Yet, as I grew,
The voices dimmed;
I thought, perhaps,
My hearing failed
Or that the caroling
Earth had simply ceased its strain,

As I assumed
The world to be
But palate for
The tongues of men . . .
Until time's passing
Disabused me of that feign.

Today, my beard
Is blanched with pearl
And I have seen,
In scores of turns,
The pulsing season's
Wheel of greens and reds and white.

So, once again
I take delight
In simple sights
Like milkweed fleece
Ablowing freely,
Calling me to second sight,

Inviting me
To see beyond
The fleece of life,
To hark the earth's
Exultant singing:
Music that I used to hear,

When as a child
My spirit roamed
As free as wind,
And Magic Earth
Revealed its cherished
Lyrics to my simple ear.

Frederick Blanch

Unsung Heroes

What senseless victories are won in hot debate . . .
       What spoils are gained?
And why expend brave, breathy soldiers
       who have been so highly trained?

Semantic cannon, firing ponderous,
       pedantic platitudes,
May still be overrun by rabbles
       of provincial attitudes.

Why launch a war of words, if no surviving tongues
       remain un-maimed,
If scourged and battered ideologies
       may persevere untamed?

The odds that nouns will drop sharp adjectives
       or scuttle their defense
Are slim, for minds, of all things, show the most
       entrenched intransigence.

Incongruous, but sending greater numbers of these
       mordant troops in battle dress
May only mean a greater likelihood that they
       will conquer less.

Yet, when we find the faultless dialectic models
       of didactics,
The verbal paladins befitting laurel,
       the masters of "syntactics,"

Do we then sing their chants, verbatim,
       to succeeding generations
And are their exploits then recounted,
       as an act of veneration?
And what distinctions shall accrue to these,

the heroes of our reason,
Intelligencers, who expose sly sophists
in eristic treason?

Shall we lament that these same conquerors
reap not demotic praise,
That neither slab nor cenotaph of stone
be chiseled with their phrase?

And yet, embattled words of truth shall be recalled
till time's last day
And their memorial shall ring from every tongue ...
as glib cliché.

Frederick Blanch

A Jar of Petals

Once, long, long ago
(Though still a fragrant memory),
Within our trysting bower
You offered me a token of your love:
A stunning orchid flower.

Later, as the love-plant died
And, sadly, one by one
Its wine-hued flowers dried,
I saved its petals
In a jar.

Now, by death possessed,
Within their glass sarcophagus
Upon my shelf, the blossoms rest . . .
Huddled, crisp and desiccate.
Amazingly, they hold their amethyst!

And when the years succeed,
(As surely they must do)
To parch my stem and crisp my leaves,
They will not pale
The color of my love for you.

For like the purple petals,
Still regal in their jar,
My love for you, unfaded,
Will transcend
My withering hour.

The Loving Cup

I am enthralled and thrilled;
I am the cup
In which your love has spilled,
Asplash to overflowing, rilled . . .
Awash in ecstasy.
My world: your face,
Enfolds me . . . tender . . . in
Your eye's embrace.
Oh, would your dainty fingers trace
My brimming rim!
Take me. Lift me
Up to heaven's gates:
Your lips,
The portals to my fates,
And quaff the drink
That never sates:
Our quenchless love.

Frederick Blanch

Requiem for a Flower

On finding a pressed flower in a favorite
book—a reminder of happier moments

What happy stories lie compressed
Within the crumbling petals
Of this flower I've pressed.

It was a precious gift from you,
My love. And like your love,
When fresh, it was a brilliant hue;

Its colors scattered rainbow light.
Your petaled emissary
Promised longed-for bliss, a living plight

Of love forever—freely given.
(I beheld it with delight.)
But now, the bloom is dark—and riven.

Like this flower, your love has died
And I have lain to rest
My happiness, along love's gelid side.

I have interred the gifts you gave:
Sweet love, bright joy, and hope . . .
Now share a common grave.

Metaphor

'T'would strain my wit past incredulity
To think a scene more beautiful:
A nest of Robins in an apple tree.
Yet, when the tree's time-wearied leaves
And feathered tenants fly,
When barren branches trace
Their secret brace
Against a lead, December sky,
Its crimson fruit long dropped
And plaintive singing
From its boughs
Long stopped,
When mud troweled by a rusty breast
Is crumbling from an empty nest,
When feathered zest has left
And apples rest in dormancy, It's then,
I realize how precious living life can be,
How much like a nest of robins
In an apple tree.
For then, incredibly, though branches stark
And heavens dark, and green leaves
Be but memory,
And echoes of a thrushy trill
Have left me pining silently,
Then, in drear December,
Then, I do remember
That spring scene of harmony
Where life has fledged and flown.
And what is life if not a song,
The taste of fruit,
And nests within a lee?
What metaphor more clear? . . .
A nest of robins in an apple tree.

Frederick Blanch

Silhouette

Its spire,
An ebon blade,
Was thrusting day's red heart;
Blind earth was quenching sunset's fire.

The lesson was too late for me.
Why did I wait till dusk,
Before I saw
The tree?

Gemini, Jekyll, or Janus?

What mask
Is that which hides
The countenance of this
Equivocating shade, I ask,

Whose smile may be reshaped by fate?
Revealing love to be ...
The other side
Of hate.

Whispers

Long, long ago, while tramping through a windblown stand of pine,
I chanced to hear what sounded like a softly whispered word
Befitting reverential prayer, within that scented shrine,
Although, its definition by the moaning wind was blurred.

However, youth joined fancy to imbue the sound with meaning,
Which I heard as dictum to record the truths of nature.
And, though another might have simply thought the wind a-keening,
I conceived the whispers as a cryptic nomenclature,

A special language, privy to the pines within the wood,
Who spoke in whispered sibilants not meant for human ear,
Who reckoned not their conversation might be understood,
Nor that their eloquence entice a mortal to their sphere.

I wrote as I perceived the pine's susurrus truths to be,
Though often fact seemed shredded as it blew through needled pine.
I strained to catch the murmurs and to note them faithfully,
Yet time intrigued to question, were the voices theirs or mine?

For did the voices speak because I wished to hear them speaking,
Did they relieve a pain, which in my ears was daily dinned?
And did my ear then hear as truth, the truths I had been seeking?
Or were both truths and voices simply whispers in the wind,

A mocking tongue, conspiracy between the breeze and pine
To veil the secret that the Mother Earth contrives to shield:
That phantom truths may not be neatly written in a line,
For scribbling speculations cannot force a shade to yield.

And though my pen has scribed no more than I considered truth,
Each day I find another of my lines I must rescind,
For age and time and walks beneath the pine confuses sooth,
Till truth seems figment of the hopes on which my dreams were pinned . . .

And all my winnowed, wishful words . . . but whispers in the wind.